Psychology

S0-CEY-946

Gillian Butler is a Consultant Clinical Psychologist at the Warneford Hospital, Oxford. After nearly ten years doing research in the Department of Psychiatry at Oxford University, she now works in the National Health Service. She is the author, with Tony Hope, of *Manage Your Mind: The Mental Fitness Guide*.

Freda McManus is a Research Cognitive Therapist in the Department of Psychiatry at Oxford University. She works on the development and evaluation of psychological treatments for anxiety disorders, and is supported by a grant from the Wellcome Trust.

Praise for *Psychology: A Very Short Introduction*

'a very readable, stimulating, and well-written introduction'
Anthony Clare

'the best available introduction to the subject'
Anthony Storr

'a brilliant introduction to the main branches of psychology'
Michael Argyle, University of Oxford

Very Short Introductions offer stimulating, accessible introductions to a wide variety of subjects, demonstrating the finest contemporary thinking about their central problems and issues.

Other Very Short Introductions available from Oxford Paperbacks

Archaeology
Paul Bahn

Buddhism
Damien Keown

Classics
Mary Beard and John Henderson

Hinduism
Kim Knott

Islam
Malise Ruthven

Literary Theory
Jonathan Culler

Judaism
Norman Solomon

Music
Nicholas Cook

Politics
Kenneth Minogue

Forthcoming from Oxford Paperbacks

The Bible
John Riches

Economics
Partha Dasgupta

The Koran
Michael Cook

Law
Stephen Guest and Jeffrey Jowell

Sociology
Steve Bruce

Social and Cultural Anthropology
John Monaghan and Peter Just

Theology
David Ford

The Stroop test illustrated on the front cover is an example of one of the inventions that has enabled psychologists to study cognitive processes. The task involves asking people to name the colour in which a word has been printed. If the word 'red' is written in red ink this simple task can be performed fast and accurately. However writing the word 'red' in another colour, such as blue, interferes with this performance. When people have to read the word 'red' written in blue but respond with the word 'blue', not with the word 'red', they find it surprisingly difficult to do. The method has been adapted for studying both cognitive processes and the relationship between cognition and emotion. Factors that interfere with colour-naming include the personal relevance of the words used, hence the Stroop task can be used, for example, to give an indication of the emotional significance of particular types of material. It was invented by R. J. Stroop in 1935, and is still in use.

A VERY SHORT INTRODUCTION

Psychology

Gillian Butler
Freda McManus

Oxford   New York
OXFORD UNIVERSITY PRESS
1998

Oxford University Press, Great Clarendon Street, Oxford OX2 6DP
Oxford New York
Athens Auckland Bangkok Bogota Bombay Buenos Aires
Calcutta Cape Town Dar es Salaam Delhi Florence Hong Kong
Istanbul Karachi Kuala Lumpur Madras Madrid Melbourne
Mexico City Nairobi Paris Singapore Taipei Tokyo Toronto Warsaw
and associated companies in
Berlin Ibadan

Oxford is a trade mark of Oxford University Press

British Library Cataloguing in Publication Data
Data available

Library of Congress Cataloging in Publication Data
Butler, Gillian.
Psychology / Gillian Butler, Freda McManus.
(A very short introduction)
Includes bibliographical references and index.
1. Psychology. I. McManus, Freda. II. Title. III. Series.
BF121.B849 1998   150—dc21   97–46352
ISBN 0–19–285323–6 (pbk.)

1 3 5 7 9 10 8 6 4 2

Typeset by Best-set Typesetter Ltd., Hong Kong
Printed and bound in Great Britain
by Mackays of Chatham PLC, Chatham

Acknowledgements

In completing this book we have many debts to acknowledge. Conversations with patients, students, colleagues, friends, and family have all played their part in helping us to think clearly about psychology. The many questions that they have posed have helped us to focus on aspects of psychology that appear to be of general interest. They have also challenged us to provide answers that reveal the exciting nature of psychology as a developing science, that fit with a fast expanding set of facts, and that can be relatively simply explained and illustrated. Inevitably we have had to leave unexplored, or merely hint at the existence of, large parts of the territory. We are grateful to those whose curiosity helped to point us in directions that they found interesting.

We would particularly like to thank our original teachers of psychology for imparting an enduring enthusiasm for the subject, and also those whose introductory books on various aspects of psychology have helped us to think better about how to make the subject accessible to others. The works of some of these have been included amongst the selection of further reading that we have recommended at the end of the book.

Without the encouragement and well-informed comments of George Miller at Oxford University Press this book would not have taken the form that it has. It is a pleasure to acknowledge the help he has given as well as his work on the whole project.

Contents

William James
John Watson
Charles Darwin
Freud.

1 What is psychology? How do you study it?

Handwritten note (top right): Freud — Finally childhood experiences that continue into adult life fucking things up.

Handwritten note: the Science of Mental Life — William James definition of Human Psy.

*I*n 1890 William James, the American philosopher and physician and one of the founders of modern psychology, defined psychology as 'the science of mental life' and this definition provides a good starting point for our understanding even today. We all have a mental life and therefore have some idea about what this means, even though it can be studied in rats or monkeys as well as in people and the concept remains an elusive one.

Like most psychologists, William James was particularly interested in human psychology, which he thought consisted of certain basic elements: thoughts and feelings, a physical world which exists in time and space, and a way of knowing about these things. For each of us, this knowledge is primarily personal and private. It comes from our own thoughts, feelings, and experience of the world, and may or may not be influenced by scientific facts about these things. For this reason, it is easy for us to make judgements about psychological matters using our own experience as a touchstone. We behave as amateur psychologists when we offer opinions on complex psychological phenomena, such as whether brain-washing works, or when we espouse as facts our opinions about why other people behave in the ways that they do: think

Handwritten note (bottom): the Body Exist in Space & Time. The mind can Transcend immediate space & time.

(EXPERIENCE)

the same thing can
Be understood
the viewed
differently —

they are being insulted, feel unhappy, or suddenly give up their jobs. However problems arise when two people understand these things differently. Formal psychology attempts to provide methods for deciding which explanations are most likely to be correct, or for determining the circumstances under which each applies. The work of psychologists helps us to distinguish between inside information which is subjective, and may be biased and unreliable, and the facts: between our preconceptions and what is 'true' in scientific terms.

Psychology, as defined by William James, is about the mind or brain, but although psychologists do study the brain, we do not understand nearly enough about its workings to be able to comprehend the part that it plays in the experience and expression of our hopes, fears, and wishes, or in our behaviour during experiences as varied as giving birth or watching a football match. Indeed, it is rarely possible to study the brain directly. So, psychologists have discovered more by studying our behaviour, and by using their observations to derive hypotheses about what is going on inside us.

Psychology is also about the ways in which organisms, usually people, use their mental abilities, or minds, to operate in the world around them. The ways in which they do this have changed over time as their environment has changed. Evolutionary theory suggests that if organisms do not adapt to a changing environment they will become extinct (hence the sayings 'adapt or die' and 'survival of the fittest'). The mind has been, and is still being, shaped by adaptive processes. This means that there are evolutionary reasons why our minds work the way that they do—for instance, the reason why we are better at detecting moving objects than stationary ones may be because this ability was useful in helping our ancestors to avoid predators. It is important for psychologists, as well as for those working in other scientific disciplines such as biology and physiology, to be aware of those reasons.

A difficulty inherent in the study of psychology is that sci-

inside information —
personal, subjective,
a persons private tape's
imprints on the Psyche —

to study
behaviour
behaviorist
Psy.

Q. is the mind in the brain.
Q. Is there a mind or simply just the brain.

Q. is it innate, it's behavior or is the more?

entific facts should be objective and verifiable but the workings of the mind are not observable in the way that those of an engine are. In everyday life they can only be perceived indirectly, and have to be inferred from what can be observed i.e. behaviour. The endeavour of psychology is much like that involved in solving a crossword puzzle. It involves evaluating and interpreting the available clues, and using what you already know to fill in the gaps. Furthermore, the clues themselves have to be derived from careful observation, based on accurate measurement, analysed with all possible scientific rigour, and interpreted using logical and reasoned arguments which can be subjected to public scrutiny. Much of what we want to know in psychology—how we perceive, learn, remember, think, solve problems, feel, develop, differ from each other, and interrelate— has to be measured indirectly, and all these activities are *multiply determined*: meaning that they are influenced by several factors rather than by a single one. For example, think of all the things that may affect your response to a particular situation (losing your way in a strange town). In order to find out which factors are the important ones, a number of other confounding factors have somehow to be ruled out.

To study Behaviour

logic & Reason

Complex interactions are the norm rather than the exception in psychology, and understanding them depends on the development of sophisticated techniques and theories. Psychology has the same goals as any other science: to describe, understand, predict, and learn how to control or modify the processes that it studies. Once these goals have been achieved it can help us to understand the nature of our experience and also be of practical value. For instance, psychological findings have been useful in fields as varied as developing more effective methods of teaching children to read, in designing control panels for machines that reduce the risk of accidents, and in alleviating the suffering of people who are emotionally distressed.

— to OBSERVE — to See — study.

OBJECTIVE & VERIFIABLE ARE UNBIASED STUDY —

to OBTAIN TRUTH & FACT

it's not as simple as studying a CAR ENGINE —

Historical background

Although psychological questions have been discussed for centuries, they have only been investigated scientifically in the past 150 years. Early psychologists relied on *introspection*, that is, the reflection on one's own conscious experience, to find answers to psychological questions. These early psychological investigations aimed to identify mental structures. But following the publication by Charles Darwin of *The Origin of Species* in 1859, the scope of psychology expanded to include the *functions* as well as the *structures* of consciousness. Mental structures and functions are still of central interest to psychologists today, but using introspection for studying them has obvious limitations. As Sir Francis Galton pointed out, it leaves one 'a helpless spectator of but a minute fraction of automatic brain work'. Attempting to grasp the mind through introspection, according to William James, is like 'turning up the gas quickly enough to see how the darkness looks'. Contemporary psychologists therefore prefer to base their theories on careful observations of the phenomena in which they are interested, such as the behaviour of others rather than on reflections upon their own experience.

In 1913 John Watson published a general behaviourist manifesto for psychology which asserted that, if psychology was to be a science, the data on which it was based must be available for inspection. This focus on observable behaviour rather than on internal (unobservable) mental events was linked with a theory of learning and an emphasis on reliable methods of observation and experimentation which still influence psychology today. The behaviourist approach suggests that all behaviour is the result of conditioning which can be studied by specifying the *stimulus* and observing the *response* to it (*S-R psychology*). What happens in between these two, the *intervening variables*, was thought unimportant by the earlier behaviourists, but has since become a prime source of experimental hypotheses. Testing hypotheses about these things has enabled psychologists to develop increasingly sophisticated theories about mental structures, functions, and processes.

Two other significant influences on the development of psychology early this century came from *Gestalt psychology* and from *psychoanalysis*. Gestalt psychologists working in Germany made some interesting observations about the ways in which psychological processes are organized. They showed that our experience differs from what would be expected if it were based solely on the physical properties of external stimuli, and concluded that 'the whole is greater than the sum of the parts'. For example, when two lights in close proximity flash in succession, what we see is one light that moves between the two positions (this is how films work). Recognizing that mental processes contribute in this way to the nature of experience laid the groundwork for contemporary developments in *cognitive psychology*, which is the branch of psychology that studies such internal processes.

Sigmund Freud's theories about the continuing influence of early childhood experiences, and about the theoretical psychological structures he named the *ego, id,* and *superego,* drew attention to *unconscious* processes. These processes, which include unconscious and unacceptable wishes and desires, are inferred, for example, from dreams, slips of the tongue, and mannerisms and are thought to influence behaviour. In particular, unconscious conflicts are hypothesized to be a prime cause of psychological distress, which psychoanalysts can help to relieve by assisting in their expression, and by using psychodynamic theories based on Freud's work to interpret patients' behaviours. The unobservable nature of the mental processes on which Freud's theories are based makes the theories difficult to test scientifically, and for many years the more scientific and the more interpretive branches of psychology developed independently, along separate routes.

Contemporary psychology is at an exciting stage today partly because these divisions are, in places, breaking down. Psychology is not the only discipline that has had to tackle questions about how we can know about things that we cannot observe directly—think of physics and biochemistry. Technological and theoretical advances have assisted this process and such developments have changed, and are continuing to change, the nature of psychology as a science. Psychologists can now use sophisticated measuring instruments, electronic equipment, and improved statistical methods to analyse multiple variables and huge quantities of data, using computers and all the paraphernalia involved in information technology. Studying the mind as an *information processing system* has enabled them to find out more about things that cannot be observed, and the many variables that intervene between stimulus and response, such as those involved in attention, thinking, and decision-making. They are now in a position to base their hypotheses about these things not solely on hypothetical theories arising from introspection, as did the early analysts, or solely on observations of behaviour, as did early behaviourists, but on combinations of these things backed up by more *reliable* and *valid* methods of observation and measurement. These developments have produced a revolution in psychology as 'the science of mental life', and their continued development means that there is still much that remains to be discovered.

Psychology as a science

Psychology is a science in that it makes use of scientific methods wherever possible, but it must also be remembered that psychology is a science at an early stage of development. Some of the things in which psychologists are interested can-

cognitive Psy } Studing the
mental
processes

not be wholly understood using scientific methods alone, and some would argue that they never will be. For example, the *humanistic* school of psychology places greater emphasis on individuals' accounts of their subjective experiences, which cannot easily be quantified or measured. Some of the main methods that are typically used by psychologists are shown in Box 1.1.

Box 1.1. *The main methods used*

Laboratory experiments: a hypothesis derived from a theory is tested under controlled conditions which are intended to reduce bias in both the selection of subjects used and in the measurement of the variables being studied. Findings should be replicable but may not generalize to more real-life settings.

Field experiments: hypotheses are tested outside laboratories, in more natural conditions, but these experiments may be less well controlled, harder to replicate, or may not generalize to other settings.

Correlational methods: assessing the strength of the relationship between two or more variables, such as reading level and attention span. This is a method of data analysis, rather than data collection.

Observations of behaviour: the behaviour in question must be clearly defined, and methods of observing it should be reliable. Observations must be truly representative of the behaviour that is of interest.

Case studies: particularly useful as a source of ideas for future research, and for measuring the same behaviour repeatedly under different conditions.

Self-report and Questionnaire studies: these provide subjective data, based on self-knowledge (or introspection), and their reliability can be ensured through good test design and by standardizing the tests on large representative samples.

Interviews and surveys: also useful for collecting new ideas, and for sampling the responses of the population in which the psychologist is interested.

— Unconscious Psy. Conflicts.
Freud - unconscious & unacceptable
wises - Desire's - Drives - sex id.
All This is un-observable & Highly Questionable

Any science can only be as good as the *data* on which it is based. Hence psychologists must be objective in their methods of data collection, analysis, and interpretation, in their use of statistics, and in the interpretation of the results of their analyses. An example will illustrate how, even if the data collected are valid and reliable, pitfalls can easily arise in the way they are interpreted. If it is reported that 90 per cent of child abusers were abused themselves as children, it is easy to assume that most people who were abused as children will go on to become child abusers themselves—and indeed such comments often reach the media. In fact, the interpretation does not follow logically from the information given—the majority of people who have themselves been abused do not repeat this pattern of behaviour. Psychologists, as researchers, have therefore to learn both how to present their data in an objective way that is not likely to mislead, and how to interpret the facts and figures reported by others. This involves a high degree of critical, scientific thinking.

The main branches of psychology

It has been argued that psychology is not a science because there is no single governing paradigm or theoretical principle upon which it is based. Rather it is composed of many loosely allied schools of thought. But this is perhaps inevitable, because of its subject matter. Studying the physiology, biology, or chemistry of an organism provides the kind of exclusive focus that is not available to psychologists, precisely because they are interested in mental processes, which cannot be separated from all the other aspects of the organism. So there are, as one might expect, many approaches to the study of psychology, ranging from the more artistic to the more scientific, and the different branches of the subject may seem at times like completely separate fields. The main branches are listed in Box 1.2.

Box 1.2. *The main branches of psychology*

Abnormal: the study of psychological dysfunctions and of ways of overcoming them.

Behavioural: emphasizes behaviour, learning, and the collection of data which can be directly observed.

Biological (and comparative): the study of the psychology of different species, inheritance patterns, and determinants of behaviour.

Cognitive: focuses on finding out how information is collected, processed, understood, and used.

Developmental: how organisms change during their lifespan.

Individual differences: studying large groups of people so as to identify and understand typical variations, for example in intelligence or personality.

Physiological: focuses on the influence of physiological state on psychology, and on the workings of the senses, nervous system, and brain.

Social: studying social behaviour, and interactions between individuals and groups

In practice there is considerable overlap between the different branches of psychology and between psychology and related fields.

Close relatives of psychology

There are some fields with which psychology is frequently confused—and indeed there are good reasons for the confusion. First, psychology is not psychiatry. Psychiatry is a branch of medicine which specializes in helping people to overcome mental disorders. It therefore concentrates on what happens when things go wrong: on mental illness and mental distress. Psychologists also apply their skills in the clinic, but they are not medical doctors and combine with their focus on psychological problems and distress a wide knowledge of normal psychological processes and development. They are not usually able to prescribe drugs; rather they specialize in helping people to understand, control, or modify their thoughts or behaviour in order to reduce their suffering and distress.

Second, psychology is often confused with psychotherapy. Psychotherapy is a broad term referring to many different types of psychological therapy, but referring to no particular one exclusively. Although the term is often used to refer to psychodynamic and humanistic approaches to therapy, it also has a wider, more general use; for example, there has recently been a great expansion of behavioural and cognitive-behavioural psychotherapy.

Third, there are many related fields in which psychologists may work, or collaborate with others, such as psychometrics, psychophysiology, psycholinguistics, and neuropsychology. Psychologists also play a part in broader, developing fields to which others contribute as well, such as cognitive science and information technology, or the understanding of psychophysiological aspects of phenomena such as stress, fatigue, or insomnia. Psychology as used in the clinic may be well known, but it is just one branch of a much bigger subject.

The aims and structure of this book

Our aim is to explain and to illustrate why psychology is interesting, important, and useful today, and therefore this book focuses on contemporary material. As most psychologists are interested in people, examples will predominantly be drawn from human psychology. Nevertheless, the book starts from the assumption that the minimum condition for having a psychology, as opposed to being a plant or an amoeba, is the possession of a mental control system (in informal terms a 'mind') that enables the organism to operate both in and on the world. Once the brain and nervous system have evolved sufficiently to be used as a control centre, there are certain things it must be able to do: pick up information about the world outside itself, keep track of that information, store it for later use, and use it to organize its behaviour so as, crudely speaking, to get more of what it wants and less of what it does not want. Different organisms do these things in different ways (for example, they have different kinds of sense organs), and yet some of the processes involved are similar across species (for example, some types of learning, and some expressions of emotion). One of the central concerns of psychologists is to find out how these things come about. So Chapters 2–5 will focus on four of the most important questions that psychologists ask: What gets into the mind? What stays in the mind? How do we use what is in the mind? and Why do we do what we do? They aim to show how psychologists find out about the processes involved in perception and attention (Chapter 2), in learning and memory (Chapter 3), in thinking, reasoning, and communicating (Chapter 4), and in motivation and emotion (Chapter 5), and attempt to explain the ways in which they work for us. These chapters focus on generalities: on the commonalities between people. They aim to describe our 'mental furniture', and to look at some of the hypotheses psychologists have made and at a few of the models they have constructed to explain their observations.

Psychologists are also interested in the differences between people and in the determinants of their obvious variety. If we are going to understand people better we need to disentangle general influences from individual ones. If there were only general patterns and rules, and we all had the same mental furniture, then all people would be psychologically identical, which obviously they are not. So how do we explain how they come to be the way they are, and how do we understand their differences, their difficulties, and their interactions? Chapter 6 asks: Is there a set pattern of human development? Chapter

7 is about individual differences and asks: Can we categorize people into types? Chapter 8 asks: What happens when things go wrong? and focuses on abnormal psychology, and Chapter 9 asks: How do we influence each other? and describes social psychology. Finally, in Chapter 10 we ask 'What is psychology for?', describe the practical uses to which psychology has been put, and offer some speculations about the types of advance that might be expected in the future.

Reference

James, W. (1890/1950). *The Principles of Psychology* (vol. i). New York, Dover.

2 What gets into our minds?
Perception

Look steadily at the drawing in Figure 2.1. This picture of a *Necker cube* is made up entirely of black lines in two-dimensional space, but what you *perceive* is a three-dimensional cube. Looking for some time at this cube produces an apparent reversal, so that the face that was in front becomes the back face of a cube facing the other way. These representations alternate even if you try not to let them do so, as the brain attempts to make sense of an ambiguous drawing with insufficient information to settle

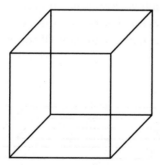

Figure 2.1. Necker cube

for one interpretation or the other. It seems that perception is not just a matter of passively picking up information from the senses, but the product of an active construction process.

Even more confusing is the drawing of the devil's tuning fork (Figure 2.2) which misleads us by using standard cues for depth perception. Alternately we see, or cannot see, a three-dimensional representation of a three-pronged fork. Similar phenomena can be demonstrated using other senses. If you repeat the word 'say' to yourself quickly and steadily you will alternately hear 'say say say . . . ' and 'ace ace ace . . . '. The point is the same: the brain works on the information received and makes hypotheses about reality without our conscious direction, so that what we are ultimately aware of is a combination of *sensory stimulation* and *interpretation*. If we are driving in thick fog, or trying to read in the dark, then the guesswork becomes obvious: 'Is this our turning or a driveway?'; 'Does it say "head" or "dead"?' Sensory processes partly determine what gets into our minds, but we can already see that other more hidden and complex processes also contribute to what we perceive.

We generally assume that the world is as we see it and that others see it the same way—that our senses reflect an objective and shared reality. We assume that our senses represent the world in which we live as accurately as a mirror reflects the face that peers into it, or as a camera creates a snapshot of a particular instant, frozen in time. Of course if our senses did

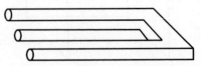

Figure 2.2. The devil's tuning fork

not provide us with somewhat accurate information we could not rely on them as we do, but nevertheless psychologists have found that these assumptions about perception are misleading. Picking up information about our worlds is not a passive, reflective process, but a complex, active one in which the mind and the senses work together, helping us to construct a *perception of* reality. We do not just see patterns of light, dark, and colour—we organize these patterns of stimulation so that we see objects that have meaning for us. We can name or recognize them, and identify them as entirely new or similar to other objects. As we shall see throughout this book, the subject matter of psychology is never simple, and some of its commonest problems are illustrated by the work on perception. First we have to determine which are the relevant factors (sensation, interpretation, and attention are three in this case), then attempt to understand, and construct theories to explain, the ways in which they interact.

Most psychological research into perception has concentrated on visual perception, because vision is our best developed sense: about half the *cortex* (the convoluted grey matter in the brain) is related to vision. Visual examples can also be illustrated, so they will predominate in this chapter.

Perceiving the real world

The first stage of perception involves detecting the signal that something is out there. The human eye can detect only a minute fraction of 1 per cent of all electromagnetic energy— the visible spectrum. Bees and butterflies can see ultraviolet rays, and bats and porpoises can hear sounds two octaves beyond our range. So what we know about reality is limited by the capabilities of our sense organs. Within those limitations, our sensitivity is remarkable: on a clear dark night, we could theoretically see a single candle flame 30 miles away. When we detect a signal such as a light, our sensory receptors convert one form of energy into another, so information about the light is transmitted as a pattern of neural impulses. The raw material of perception for all the senses consists of neural impulses which are channelled to differently specialized parts of the brain. For the impulses to be interpreted as seeing a candle flame, they have to reach the visual cortex and the pattern and rate of firing in activated cells and lack of firing in inhibited cells has both to be distinguished from the background level of cellular activity (or *neural noise*), and decoded. Interestingly, the ability to detect a signal accurately is far more variable than would be expected from knowledge about sensory systems alone, and is influenced by many other factors: some are obvious, like attention, others less obvious, involving our expectations, motivations, or inclinations such as a tendency to say 'yes' or 'no' when uncertain. If you are listening to the radio while waiting for an important telephone call, you may think you heard it ring when it did not, whereas if you are engrossed in the radio programme and not expecting a phone call you may completely fail to hear it ring. Such differences in detecting signals have important practical implications, for example in designing effective warning systems in intensive care units or control panels for complex machines.

Theories constructed to explain these findings enable psychologists to make and to test predictions. *Signal detection theory* suggests that accurate perception is determined not just by sensory capacity but by a combination of sensory processes and decision processes. Decisions vary according to the degree of cautiousness required (or *response bias*) in use at the time. A laboratory technician scanning slides for cancerous cells responds to every anomaly and sorts out the 'false alarms' later, but a driver deciding when to overtake the car in front must get it right each time or risk a collision. Measures of sensitivity and of cautiousness can be calculated by counting 'hit rates' and 'false alarms' and applying relatively simple statistical procedures, to predict when a signal (a cancerous cell, or an oncoming car) will be accurately detected. These measures are demonstrably reliable, and have many practical uses, for example in training air traffic controllers, whose decisions about the presence or absence of a radar signal may make the difference between a safe landing and a disaster.

All senses respond better to changes in the environment than to a steady state, and receptors stop responding altogether, or *habituate*, when nothing changes, so you notice the noise of the fridge when it switches on but not later. In our busy lives one might suppose that rest from sensory stimulation would be a boon, but *sensory deprivation*, or the absence of all sensory stimulation, can induce frightening and bizarre experiences including hallucinations in some people. The degree of distress experienced varies according to what people expect. The same applies if the senses are overloaded for a significant length of time. As people who have recently been to pop concerts, football matches, or especially busy supermarkets will testify, these can be stimulating, exhausting, or confusing experiences.

Perceptual organization

Organized perception, which enables us to discern patterns in what we perceive so as to make sense of it, happens so naturally and effortlessly that it is hard to believe it is a substantial achievement. Computers can be programmed to play chess, but they cannot yet be programmed to match even relatively rudimentary visual skills. The main principles of perceptual organization were discovered by the Gestalt psychologists in the 1930s.

Look at the Rubin's vase (Figure 2.3). You will see either a vase or two silhouettes, but not both at once. If you look at the vase the silhouettes disappear, becoming the ground against

Figure 2.3. Rubin's vase

which the figure stands out, but seeing the silhouettes as figures turns the 'vase' into background. *Figure-ground perception* is important because it forms the basis for much of the rest of the way that we see things. Three of the other Gestalt principles of organization, those of similarity, proximity, and closure, are illustrated in Figure 2.4. Perceptually we group together things that are similar or close to each other (*a* and *b*) and fill in the gaps if shown an incomplete figure (*c*). These organizing principles help us to identify objects and to separate them from their surroundings. We usually identify the most important figures first and explore details later, so in Figure 2.5 we see H before S. Whether or not perceptual processing always proceeds in this order is still uncertain. The point is that one of the things we contribute to the construction of our own reality is a systematic way of organizing the information received.

Gestalt psychologists believe that our ability to identify objects visually, and to distinguish them from their background, is innate rather than learned. From recordings of single cells in the brain it appears that some cells respond most to lines having a specific orientation or length, and others may detect simple shapes or surfaces. Are we born with such specialized detectors, or do they develop later? Adults who were blind at birth but subsequently gained their sight, for example follow-

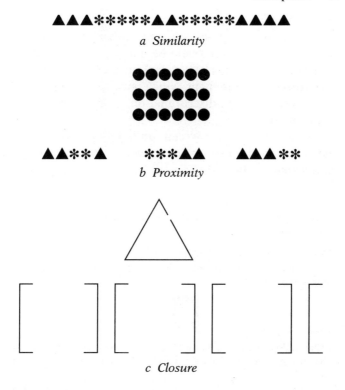

a Similarity

b Proximity

c Closure

Figure 2.4. Gestalt principles of similarity, proximity, and closure

```
S           S
S           S
S           S
SSSSSSSSSS
S           S
S           S
S           S
```

Figure 2.5. Seeing H before S

ing the surgical removal of cataracts, have all found visual perception extremely difficult, and continue to make visual errors. Although there could be many reasons for this, it seems that visual skills have to be learned. For example, animals reared in diffuse light, which preserves the optic nerve but prevents pattern discrimination, tend subsequently to bump into things.

The extent to which perception is influenced by stored knowledge and the expectations created by this knowledge is remarkable (see Box 2.1).

Box 2.1. *Perceptual set: what you know influences what you see*

Subjects were shown sets of letters or numbers which they had to name out loud as they appeared. Then they were shown the following ambiguous figure:

$$\mathsf{I3}$$

This could be read as a B or a 13. If it followed a series of letters it was named as a B, but if it followed a series of numbers it was named as a 13.

Bruner and Minturn, 1955

Creating a *perceptual set* (an expectation that guides perception) makes it easier to perceive something belonging to that set—which is why the 'own brand' items in a supermarket will be easier to find if they look similar to each other and different from rival brands.

Paying attention: making use of a limited capacity system

Perception involves more than the acquisition of discriminatory skills. It also involves forming hypotheses, making decisions, and applying organizing principles. Most of the time these things go on outside awareness and sometimes we can even be unaware that we have perceived, or chosen to perceive, anything at all. This is because what gets into the mind is determined by the way our perceptual system works and also by the way in which we select from amongst the many things that demand our attention. Our brains are limited capacity systems, and to make the best use of them it helps to direct our attention appropriately. If you set a tape recorder running at a noisy party you would most likely hear something resembling a confused babble. But if you start talking —or paying attention—to someone at the party, your conversation will stand out against the background noise and you may not even know whether the person behind you was talking in French or English. Yet if someone mentions your name, without even raising their voice, you will be highly likely to notice it. Normally, we focus as we wish by filtering out what does not matter to us at the time, on the basis of *low level information*, such as the voice of the speaker or direction from which the voice comes.

Noticing our own name is a puzzling exception to this rule, and several explanations have been suggested for how the filter system works. We must know something about those things we ignore or we would not know that we wanted to ignore them. Perceiving something without realizing that we have done so has been called *subliminal perception* (Box 2.2). Laboratory studies have shown that our attentional processes can work so fast and efficiently that they can protect us from consciously noticing things that might upset us, such as obscene or disturbing words.

Paying attention is one way in which we select what gets into our minds—but we do not have to pay attention to only one thing at a time. In fact, divided attention is the norm. We can divide our attention most easily between information coming to us through different channels—which is why I can

keep an eye on the stew while peeling the potatoes and listening to the children. I can even worry about the letter from the
bank manager at the same time, but there are limits to my ver-
satility. Air traffic controllers were once trained to do many
things simultaneously: watch a radar screen, talk to pilots,
track different flight paths, and read messages handed to
them on paper. Provided the flow of traffic was manageable
they could divide their attention in all these ways at once.
However, during the development of safety systems, simu-
lated tests of their capacity showed that if the flow of information was too great, or if they were tired, their responses
became disorganized and even quite bizarre: standing up and
pointing out directions to pilots thousands of feet up in the air
and many miles away, or shouting loudly to get the information across.

Box 2.2. *Subliminal perception: a means of self-protection?*

Two spots of light are shown on a screen, and in one of them a word
is written so faintly that it cannot be consciously perceived. Subjects
judge the brightness of the spots as dimmer when there is an emotional word hidden in the light than when the word is pleasant or
neutral. This has been called *perceptual defence* because it potentially can protect us from unpleasant stimuli.

It will be no surprise to learn that attention is a sensitive
process. Many factors have been found to interfere with it,
such as similarity between stimuli, difficulty of the task, lack
of skill or practice, distress or worry, preoccupation or absent-mindedness, drugs, boredom, and sensory habituation.
One reason why it is safer to use railways to transport people
through a long underground tunnel such as the one under the
channel between France and England, is that driving would
be too risky. Without sufficient sensory variety perceptual
systems habituate and attention wanders. We adapt, or habituate to stimuli that do not change, and orient towards

something new. So lying quite still in the bath I will not notice the gradual temperature change until I suddenly move about.

What we actually perceive, in combining perception and attention, is thus influenced by internal factors such as emotions and bodily states as well as by external factors. People who fear social rejection more readily notice signs of unfriendliness than of friendliness, such as negative facial expressions, and hungry people judge pictures of food as more brightly coloured than pictures of other things. These findings confirm that so much of perception goes on outside awareness that we cannot be sure that there is a good match between what we perceive and reality, or between what we perceive and what others perceive. Psychologists have suggested that two kinds of processing are involved.

- *Bottom-up processing* starts when we see something out in the real world which triggers a set of internal cognitive processes. This 'stimulus-driven' processing reflects our responsiveness to the outside world, and tends to prevail when viewing conditions are good.
- *Top-down processing* reflects this contribution of conceptually driven, central processes. Even when reacting to light or sound waves each of us brings past experience (and attention) to the task, and if the viewing conditions are poor, or our expectations are strong, we will rely more on internal and less on external information.

Glance at the triangle on p. 24 (Figure 2.6) to see what it says. Did you notice the error? Most people do not do so at first, as their expectations about the well-known phrase (top-down processing) interfere with accurate perception (bottom-up processing).

Contemporary theories of perception have changed to take such observations into account. For example, Ulric Neisser suggested that we use 'schemas' built up from past experience to make sense of the world: our past experience leads us to

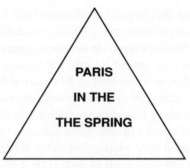

Figure 2.6

form expectations about objects or events (schemas), and we use these schemas to anticipate what we are likely to encounter. Our schemas, which have been developing since infancy, direct our exploration of the perceptual world, so we sample incoming information, and modify schemas according to what we find. According to this view, perception is a continuous active cycle, rather than a one-way process or a passive snapshot of what is there (Figure 2.7). What we anticipate or expect affects what we perceive, but what is actually

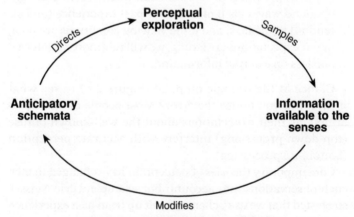

Figure 2.7. Neisser's perceptual cycle

there affects what we anticipate. Imagine you are meeting a friend in a crowd. You expect he will look much the same as usual so you look out for a tall man with a beard and ignore short, clean-shaven ones. Suddenly your friend taps you on the shoulder. You have missed him because he shaved off his beard. If you modify your schema accordingly you may not miss him next time. So our expectations are continually changing and adjusting as we take in new information, and our perceptual system helps us to adapt in ways that some other animals cannot do. A frog catches a fly by perceiving its movement, and will die of starvation if surrounded by stationary (but edible) dead flies.

Learning from perceptual impairment: the man who mistook his wife for a hat

The complexities of perception mean that it can go wrong in many different ways. In *The Man Who Mistook His Wife for a Hat* Oliver Sacks describes what happens when more complex, interpretive perceptual abilities are seriously impaired. His patient was a talented musician, with no deterioration in his musical or other mental abilities. He was aware that he made mistakes, particularly in recognizing people, but not otherwise aware that anything much was wrong. He could converse normally, but no longer recognize his students, and confused inanimate objects (such as his shoe) with animate ones (his foot). At the end of an interview with Dr Sacks he looked for his hat, but instead reached for, and tried to lift off, his wife's head. He could not recognize the emotional expressions or the sex of people seen on TV, and could not identify members of his family from their photographs, even though he could do so by their voices. Sacks reports that 'visually he was lost in a world of lifeless abstractions', as if he had lost an important organizing principle. He could see the world as a computer construes it, by means of key features and schematic relationships, so that when asked to identify a glove he described it as 'a container of some sort' and as 'a continuous surface infolded on itself [which] appears to have five outpouchings . . . ' (p. 13). This severe perceptual impairment affected visual recognition more than other things: as if he could see without understanding or interpreting what he saw. Bereft of the interpretive aspect of perception, he came to a complete stop if he had to rely on visual information alone, but was able to keep going by humming to himself—by living in the musical, auditory world for which he was especially skilled. Although he could make hypotheses (about his wife's head or the glove)—as indeed we do when looking at the Necker cube (Figure 2.1), he could not make judgements about those things. Studying carefully the selective impairment of high-level perceptual functions provides clues that help us to understand many things: the part that those functions play, not only in perception but in helping us to live in the real world; which functions are separately coded in the brain and where the organization of those functions is located.

So perception is the end product of complex processes, many of which take place out of awareness. Psychologists have now learned so much about perception that they can simulate a visual environment sufficiently accurately for trainee surgeons to use *'virtual reality'* to practise doing complex operations. Virtual reality creates the illusion of three-dimensional space, so that it becomes possible to reach round something or pass through 'solid' objects at the touch of a button. Perceptual systems are able to learn and adapt so quickly, however, that being able to do this is a mixed blessing. Surgeons who have practised like this sufficiently long to readjust their use of standard perceptual cues for moving around safely in three-dimensional space are especially prone to car accidents afterwards.

This introduction to the field of perception only starts to

answer questions about what gets into the mind. The subject covers many more fascinating topics ranging from ideas about perceptual development to debates about the degree to which the processes involved in perception are automatic or can be intentionally controlled. The aim has been to illustrate the point that reality as we know it is partly an individual, human construction. Each of us makes it up as we go along, and psychologists help us to understand many of the conditions which determine how we do this. Knowing something about what gets into the mind we can go on to ask how much of it stays there, to become the basis for what we learn and remember.

References

Bruner, J. S., and Minturn, A. L. (1995). 'Perceptual identification and perceptual organization'. *Journal of General Psychology*, 53: 21–31.

Sacks, O. (1985). *The Man Who Mistook His Wife for a Hat*. London, Gerald Duckworth & Co. Ltd. (Picador, 1986).

3 What stays in the mind?
Learning and Memory

*W*hen you learn something it makes a difference. There is something you can do that you could not do before, like play the piano, or there is something that you now know that you did not know before, like what 'empirical' means. When something stays in the mind, we assume it is stored somewhere, and we call this storage system 'memory'. The system does not work perfectly: we sometimes have to 'rack our brains' or 'search our memories', but perhaps the most common preconception about what stays in the mind is that there is a place where it is all stored. Sometimes one cannot find what one wants, but it is probably there somewhere if only one knew where to look. But psychologists' discoveries about learning and memory demonstrate that what is stored in the mind cannot be adequately understood by using the analogy of the repository.

About memory, William James asked in 1890: 'why should this absolute god-given Faculty retain so much better the events of yesterday than those of last year, and, best of all, those of an hour ago? Why, again, in old age should its grasp of childhood's events seem firmest? Why should repeating an experience strengthen our recollection of it? Why should drugs, fevers, asphyxia, and excitement resuscitate things long since forgotten? . . . such peculiarities seem quite fantastic; and might, for aught we can see *a priori*, be the precise opposites of what they are. Evidently, then, *the faculty does not exist absolutely, but works under conditions;* and *the quest of the conditions* becomes the psychologist's most interesting task.' (*Principles of Psychology*, i. 3).

Understanding what stays in the mind still presents challenges to psychologists. Their studies have revealed many odd facts. For example, both experimental work and clinical observations show that memories for distant events have different characteristics from memories for recent events. People suffering from amnesia may retain childhood memories but find it almost impossible to acquire new memories—such as the names of people they have just met. Or they may remember how to tell the time but not remember what year it is, or be able to learn the layout of a new home. For some, new learning appears to be impossible, even though they can accurately describe their childhoods and repeat back to you a line of poetry you have just recited. They may readily learn new motor skills like typing, yet deny having ever seen a word processor before. Although the source of the damage in such cases appears to be located in a specific part of the brain (the hippocampus), no 'storeroom' where neural connections, or networks of interconnected 'wires' terminate, has been found. The processes of learning and memory, which we use unthinkingly every day, are thus intimately connected and so complex that it has not yet proved possible to build a computer capable of simulating them accurately.

We will start with learning, to illustrate how psychologists understand the different ways in which learning 'makes a difference'.

Learning

We tend to assume that the ability to learn is determined by such things as how clever you are, whether you pay attention, and whether you persist when the going gets tough. But it turns out that there are different kinds of learning, many of which do not involve conscious effort or formal instruction. We are learning all the time, even if we are not attempting to do so, and some of the ways in which we learn are similar to the ways in which other animals learn, despite our greater capacity. Human learning is triggered in a number of different ways. The environments into which babies are born vary so enormously even in basics, such as how they are handled, fed, and kept warm, that adaptation is essential. Babies adapt so fast and so well because they are predisposed to learn, and because they respond particularly strongly to certain types of events: *contingencies*—what goes together with what; *discrepancies*—differences from the norm; and *transactions*—interactions with others.

Learning about contingencies allows one to make things happen: turn the tap and the water (usually) runs. By learning how to turn the tap on and off we learn how to control the flow of water. Tiny babies repeatedly explore contingencies: waving their arms about, they hit something that makes a noise and do this over and over again, until they can control the noise they make. This apparent fascination with contingencies is an important basis for other types of learning such as skill learning. Once you have mastered a skill you can do it without thinking and turn your attention to something else: when you can read words effortlessly you can think about their meaning. If you can play the tune automatically you can think about how to interpret the music.

Once you know what to expect, then discrepancies become fascinating—provided they are not too radical. Small changes in a child's world (a new type of food, sleeping in a different place) invite exploration and help the child to learn, but if everything is suddenly disrupted then the child becomes seriously distressed. In the same way, different ways of singing the song (playing the game) become interesting once you know its basic pattern. This ability to learn by making distinctions is lasting and fundamental. Older people are better at new learning when they already have relevant stored knowledge and are therefore noticing and adjusting to discrepancies, but worse at learning something completely new.

Transactions with others are necessary for survival for a human infant, and the way babies participate in these transactions, at first by crying and looking, and later by smiling and in more complex ways, enables them to learn about and control their worlds. A baby that cries when it needs something is engaged (however unknowingly) in a participation which influences others. It is not engaged in a power struggle, manipulating people for attention, but initiating a transaction that will help it to survive. If nobody responds, the baby eventually gives up and becomes apathetic, as if it had learned that there was no point. Babies (and indeed adults too) are particularly responsive to *contingencies*, *discrepancies*, and *transactions*, and these events trigger some of the basic processes involved in learning.

Perhaps the most basic of the many different kinds of learning is *association learning* or *conditioning*. *Classical conditioning* was first explored and understood by Pavlov, working with dogs in the 1920s. Having found a way of measuring their salivation in response to food he noticed that the dogs started to salivate before they were given the food. The reflexive, or *unconditioned response*, of salivation was triggered by things associated with the food, like the sight of the bowl, the person who brought the food, or the sound of the bell that was paired with the food (rung as the food appeared). Pavlov thought that virtually any stimulus could become a *conditioned stimulus* for salivation—the sound of a metronome, a triangle drawn on a large card, and even an electric shock, and he concluded that learning takes place when a previously neutral stimulus (a bell) is associated with an *unconditioned stimulus* (something to which we naturally respond, such as food). The variants, determinants, and limits of classical conditioning have been minutely studied, so we know how conditioned responses die away, or generalize to similar things; how emotions can be conditioned (a child's fear of the waves), and counter-conditioned (by holding a parent's hand while paddling) and new associations can be made quite dramatically in 'one-trial learning', as when a particular food makes you sick and you never want to touch it again.

Operant conditioning, first investigated by B. F. Skinner, explains the part played by *reinforcement* in learning. Operant conditioning provides a powerful means of controlling what people (and animals) learn and what they do. The main idea is that if an action is followed by a pleasant effect it will be repeated—whether performed by a man or a rat. If pressing a lever brings with it a food pellet, a rat will learn to press the lever. The hungrier it is the faster it will learn, and the strength of its response can be precisely predicted by the rate at which the food pellets are dispensed. The rat will 'work' hardest if the pellets arrive intermittently and unpredictably (which is how fruit machines keep us hooked), and less hard if the pellets arrive after the same amount of time whatever the rat does. Hence, people paid at a constant rate for doing boring, repetitive work quickly lose motivation in comparison to those paid piece-rate. Using the principles of reinforcement, extraordinary feats of learning have been demonstrated, such as teaching pigeons to 'play' table tennis with their beaks by *shaping* their behaviour gradually in the right direction.

Operant conditioning has many practical applications. If you want a response to continue after it has been learned, such as getting a child to tidy its room, you should reward it intermittently, not continuously. If you occasionally reward a behaviour you want to decrease rather than increase (for example, angry outbursts, tantrums) you will strengthen the behaviour by mistake. If a reward arrives too late, it will be far less effective (thanking an employee a week after you received their report rather than immediately). Reinforcement thus provides the fuel for the learning machine, which works equally well whether the reinforcer is positive, in that it provides something pleasant, or negative, in that it takes away something unpleasant. If you miss the show you learn to plan ahead.

Skinner had strong views about punishment, which is easy to confuse with, but very different from, negative reinforcement. He believed that it was an ineffective way of helping people to learn because it is painful but uninformative. It works by discouraging a particular kind of behaviour without suggesting what to do instead. In fact, punishment raises complex issues. It can be effective, for example in reducing the self-injurious behaviour of some disturbed children, and it can be administered in mild but effective ways (a spray of water in the face, or *time-out* from the situation). But its effects may be temporary, or only effective in specific circumstances (adolescents may smoke with their friends but not in front of their parents). Punishment is not often easy to deliver immediately, it conveys little information, and may be unintentionally rewarding—a teacher's reprimand to one naughty pupil may attract reinforcing kinds of attention from others in the class.

Operant principles have been turned into effective *behaviour modification* techniques in many settings such as schools, hospitals, and prisons. Theoretically they provide the power to predict and control the behaviour of others. Using this power for the purpose of toilet training is one thing, but using it for political purposes is another. One reason why this sort of abuse of power may not be the risk that was once feared is that there is room, psychologically speaking, for an element of determinism and for an element of free will in the sequence of events that lead up to a person's actions. Association learning is not the only possibility. If you notice that an advertiser is associating a new car with sexual potency, you can decide to take it or leave it on more rational grounds. If someone is nice to you for non-genuine motives you may not find the contact rewarding, so the *contingency* may fail. Clearly, we can use other types of learning, and other cognitive abilities as well.

Observational learning, learning by imitating or watching others, provides a short cut, which bypasses the need for trial and error and immediate reinforcement on which association learning depends. Much of the learning that takes place in schools is of this type, and it can also explain how we acquire attitudes and information about the social conventions of the community in which we live (see Box 3.1)

Box 3.1. *Observational learning: when others set a bad example*

Young children watched someone playing with some toys, in real life, on film, or as shown in a cartoon. Sometimes the person hit one of the dolls. The children were then taken to the same playroom, to play with the toys, and some were frustrated by the experimenter removing the toy a child was playing with. Frustrated children tended to imitate the aggressive behaviour they had observed, and copied real life models more closely than filmed or cartoon models. Further studies show that children are more likely to imitate models similar to themselves (children of the same age and sex), and people they admire.

Bandura and Walters, 1963

Latent learning is learning that does not show up straight away. If you have looked at a map of a new city, or have travelled through it as a passenger, you will learn your way around it faster than someone who is completely new to it, and your learning advantage can be accurately measured. *Insight learning* occurs when you suddenly see the solution to a prob-

lem: how to fix the broken lamp. The understanding sometimes comes in a flash, and it is not clear whether it is purely
the result of previous learning or whether it involves mentally
combining old responses in new ways, as we do when we use
the words in our language in new combinations so as to express our own ideas.

Cognitive theories of learning have moved away from the
associationist view and tried to explain the influences of other
processes, such as attention, imagination, thinking, and feeling. As soon as we start to look at the ways in which new learning interacts with what is already in the mind the distinction
between learning and memory becomes blurred. Memory,
like perception, is an active process and not just a tape record-
ing of all that you have learned. The more use you make of the
material you learn (reading a French newspaper, speaking
and writing to a French friend, watching French films, revis-
ing your grammar), the more you will remember. Material
that is passively imbibed is easily forgotten and the differences that learning makes to what stays in the mind can
be more fully understood by exploring the determinants
of what we remember—by finding out how our memory
works.

Memory

The big issue about memory is still 'how does it work?' The
following findings illustrate some of the difficulties. As early
as 1932 Sir Frederic Bartlett showed that remembering is not
just a question of making an accurate record of the information we receive, but involves fitting the new information into
what is already there and creating a narrative that makes
sense (see Box 3.2).

Bartlett argued that the process of retrieval involves reconstruction, which is influenced by the frameworks that people
already have in their heads. So memory, just like perception,

Box 3.2. *'The War of the Ghosts'*

Bartlett read people an American Indian legend, following which partly depended on understanding of unfamiliar beliefs about a spiritual world, and found that the errors they made when remembering it were not random, but systematic. In the legend, someone watches a battle involving ghosts, recounts what he saw to others, and then suddenly succumbs to a wound received from a ghost. People made sense of the unfamiliar material by fitting it into their pre-existing ideas and cultural expectations. For example, 'something black came out of his mouth' was reproduced as 'escaping breath' or 'foamed at the mouth', and the people in the story were assumed to be members of a clan called 'The Ghosts'. Also, the changes they made when remembering the story fitted with the reactions and emotions they experienced when they first heard it. One subject said, 'I wrote out the story mainly by following my own images'.

Bartlett, 1932

is both selective and interpretive. It involves construction as well as reconstruction.

We are able to recall the meaning of events far more accurately than their details, and the meaning we give to them influences the details we remember. At the time of the Watergate trials, the psychologist Ulric Neisser compared tape recordings of conversations held in the White House with reports of these conversations from one of the witnesses, John Deane, who had an exceptionally good memory. He found that the meaning of Deane's memories was accurate but that the details, including some especially 'memorable' phrases, were not. Deane was right about what happened, but wrong about the words used and the order in which topics were discussed.

At particularly important or emotional moments details tend to get better 'fixed' in our memories. However, even then the details remembered by two people present at the same event may be strikingly different. If I faced the blue sea and my husband faced the dark forest when we decided to marry each other, twenty years later we can argue about where we were at the time, and accuse each other of forgetting important shared memories, because one of us remembers the darkness and the other remembers the light. 'The past [. . .] is always an argument between counterclaimants' (Cormac McCarthy, *The Crossing*, p. 411).

How we decide between counterclaimants is still an important issue. It is possible that people brought up in painful and distressing circumstances, in which they felt neglected or victimized, later remember accurately the meaning to them of the events in their childhoods, but are incorrect about the details. This could explain some instances of *false memory syndrome* in which people are said to 'recover memories', for example of being abused in some way as small children, that turn out not to be accurate. It is also possible that the details of unusual or intense experiences *are* accurately remembered. The mistake is to believe that remembering details and believing that those details are accurate prove that the memories are correct.

Even when we do remember details accurately, the details we remember are not fixed in our memories, but remain changeable. If I witnessed an accident at a junction and am later questioned about details of what happened, such as whether the car stopped before or after the tree, I am likely to insert a tree into my memory even if there was none. Once that tree has been inserted it seems to become part of the original memory, so that I can no longer tell the difference between my 'real' memory and what I remember remembering later. So memories once told can be changed by the telling, and questions asked of witnesses in court ('did you see *a* broken head lamp' vs. 'did you see *the* broken head lamp') affect what is recalled without people knowing that this has happened.

People often wish for perfect, or photographic, memory.

Box 3.3. *The mind of a mnemonist*

One man was able to remember huge series of numbers or words after seeing them for only a few seconds—he could repeat them forwards or backwards even after a gap of fifteen years. This man's memory appeared to work by making the information he received meaningful. He associated each part of it with visual and other sensory images, making the elements unique and 'unforgettable'. But these images subsequently interfered so much with concentration that he could no longer perform simple activities including holding conversations, and became unable to function in his profession as a journalist. The problem was that new information, such as the words he heard others speak, set off an uncontrollable train of distracting associations.

Alexander Luria, 1968

However, being unable to forget may have its disadvantages (Box 3.3), and the creative, rather inaccurate system of remembering and forgetting that we have may be well adapted for our purposes.

How do models of memory account for findings as diverse as these? And what do they tell us about the function of memory? It has been proposed that three quite different kinds of memory store, which receive and lose track of information in different ways, are needed to account for observations about memory. The *sensory store* receives information from the senses (sights or sounds) and holds it in memory for about a second while we decide what to attend to. What we ignore is quickly lost and cannot be retrieved as it decays just as lights fade and sounds die away. One can sometimes catch an echo of what someone said when one was not paying attention, but literally a second later it has gone altogether. Paying attention to something transfers it to the *short-term store,* which has a capacity of about seven items. So we can remember a new telephone number for about as long as it takes to dial it. The short-term store has limited capacity and, once full, old information is displaced by new. However, continuing to attend to, turn over in one's mind, or rehearse information transfers it to the *long-term store*, which supposedly has unlimited capacity. This seems to imply that information in the long-term store need never be lost if only one knew how to find it. Forgetting would occur because similar memories become confused, and interfere with each other when we try to recall them. So, unless we have the mind of a mnemonist, one birthday party becomes confused with another and what we remember in the end is something about the significance of birthdays rather than exactly what happened when we were 5 or 10 or 15. General meanings are more important than details unless something marks those details for us (a 21st birthday or a surprise party).

So how can you establish what really happened? Or do we even need to? Evolutionary considerations may help to explain why memory works as it does. Our memory systems did not evolve because we need to catalogue the items and events in the world but because we need to adapt our behaviour. It seems that our minds, including our memories, adapt to fit our changing situations. There are things we need to remember, like how to read, what our friends are like, and what we have got to do next, and things we do not need to remember, like precise details of our past. Being hungry helps us to remember to buy something to eat, which is adaptive; if we are depressed, sad memories spring easier to mind, which may or may not be adaptive. It seems that having fragmentary memories, from which we can select according to our interests, and which we can organize in creative and useful ways is sufficient. With a few cues, reminders or partial fragments in mind, we can select, interpret, and integrate one thing with another so as to make use of what we learn and remember.

Thinking along these lines has led contemporary psychologists to think of memory as an activity, not a thing—or as a set of activities involving complex encoding and retrieval systems, some of which are now amenable to separate study. These systems, like the perceptual system described in Chapter 2, employ organizing principles. Information stays in the mind more easily if, for example, it is *relevant*, *distinctive* in some way, has been *elaborated upon* or worked with, and processed meaningfully as opposed to superficially. Organizing information we want to remember confers an advantage when it comes to remembering it (thinking of 'picnic food', or 'school lunches' as you walk round the supermarket). Some general principles of organization have been discovered, but at the same time each of us develops a personal organizational system based on past experience. So we encode, or organize incoming information differently, and have different priorities or interests when retrieving it. This helps us to adapt in the present: to avoid the people we find boring and to seek out the kind of work that feels satisfying. But it also means that our memories are not just 'snapshots' of the past. Just as we saw that perceiving and attending to the outside world helps us to construct a view of reality, so we now see that learning and memory are also active, constructive processes. Furthermore, the accuracy of our memories may be irrelevant for many purposes. In order to make the best use of what stays in the mind, it may be more important to remember meanings, and to learn to how find out the details, than to remember precisely what happened.

References

Bandura, A., and Walters, R. H. (1963). *Social Learning and Personality Development.* Orlando, Fla., Holt, Rhinehart & Winston.

Bartlett, F. C. (1932). *Remembering.* Cambridge, Cambridge University Press.

Luria, A. R. (1968). *The Mind of a Mnemonist* (trans. L. Soltaroff). New York, Basic Books.

4 How do we use what is in the mind? Thinking, Reasoning, and Communicating

*B*ehaving thoughtlessly, not stopping to think, being unreasonable or illogical, and being unable to express oneself are failings to which everyone is susceptible. The assumption is that when we do these things we are *failing*: we *should* think before we act, be thoughtful and reasonable, and be able to put straightforward thoughts into words. The skills involved in thinking, reasoning, and communicating have produced literature, medicines, the microchip, and meals for the family, and without them we would be unable to function in the ways that we do. But the mind, as we have already seen, is a creative instrument and not just a passive recipient of external information which it faithfully records, stores, and analyses, and it does not always operate according to the strict rules of logic. The investigations of psychologists show us that *cognitive skills* such as thinking, reasoning, and communicating are not merely products of rationality, and their value to us and the efficiency with which they work are not measured solely by the standards of rationality.

As the emphasis in psychology has shifted away from the study of behaviour and focused more on internal processes, the study of cognition has been approached from three angles: cognitive psychologists have developed increasingly sophisticated, laboratory-based, experimental methods; cognitive scientists have produced computer programmes to create and test artificially 'intelligent' machines, and neuropsychologists have studied cognitive processes in brain-damaged patients. In this chapter we shall see that all three approaches have furthered our understanding of human cognition.

In order to think we must have something to think with. In Chapters 2 and 3 it was argued that the 'raw material', what gets into the mind and what stays there subsequently, is not solely determined by the nature of objective reality, but also by the organization of our perceptual and attentional abilities, and by the processes involved in learning and remembering. If we can organize our perceptions so that they make sense, recall information when it is needed, and use it to think, reason, and communicate with, then we can make plans, have ideas, solve problems, imagine more or less fantastic possibilities, and tell others all about it. Psychologists are still finding out more about how we do these things.

Thinking: the building blocks

Our understanding of *concepts*, the building blocks for thought that help us to organize our thinking and to respond appropriately to our experiences, comes from the work of philosophers and linguists as well as psychologists. Concepts are abstractions that simplify and summarize what we know; they contain general as well as specific information. For example, potatoes, carrots, and leeks are all vegetables that can be cooked and eaten. If we are told that celeriac is a vegetable, using this concept tells us (roughly) what to do with it. Concepts are formed through direct contact with objects and situations, and through contact with symbols, or signs for those objects and situations, such as letters and words. I can learn about cassava by eating, growing, or reading about it.

Using concepts allows us to represent what we know in symbols—to make one thing stand for another—so a 'T' can represent a sound made in speech, and the sign 'T' can also be used to represent something the same shape: a T-junction, T-bar, or T-shirt. Some concepts are more useful to us in everyday life than others (potato rather than vegetable or chip), and these 'basic concepts' are learned faster than those that are supposedly superordinate or subordinate to them. But even concrete concepts are surprisingly imprecise or 'fuzzy'. Carrots are definitely vegetables, but tomatoes or pumpkins may not be. One theory proposes that we organize concepts around a prototype, or set of characteristic features, and psychologists have found that the more an object differs from such a prototype the harder it is to learn, remember and recognize. *Prototype theory* has been useful in revealing some of the ways in which concrete concepts influence aspects of our thinking, but it accounts less well for our use of abstract concepts, such as 'talent', which may have no obvious prototype.

We tend to suppose that our conscious mind is in control most of the time. We think about what we are doing, solve problems, and make deliberate choices such as what to wear, eat, or say. We can also describe what we have done and reflect upon our activities, hopes, and fears. We suppose that, unlike the squirrel which seeks 'unthinkingly' for its hoard of nuts when woken by the warmth of spring, we consciously think about, control, and monitor our behaviour, and that doing so makes us into 'thoughtful' or 'rational' beings. The research carried out by cognitive psychologists over the last twenty-five years has now shown that many different processes go on beneath the surface when we think, and has changed our assumptions about the conscious, logical nature of thinking.

Thinking is not, for example, always a helpful thing to do. After prolonged practice some activities that once demanded careful thought, like typing or driving a car, become automatic and can be carried out simultaneously with other activities, like having a conversation or planning a holiday. We can do them 'without thinking', and if you ask an expert typist where on the keyboard to find a particular letter that person has to make a conscious effort, and may mimic the relevant movements, in order to answer your question. Subconscious mental activities can (sometimes) be brought into consciousness, if necessary. But thinking consciously about activities that have become automatic (changing gear, running downstairs) is remarkably disruptive. Relegating them to the subconscious increases efficiency, allowing us to do them without thinking even at the cost of occasional absent-mindedness—putting the frozen peas in the bread bin, or driving home and forgetting to make a planned detour to the postbox on the way. It leaves spare thinking capacity for more important matters. The study of such *cognitive failures* shows that they increase with stress, fatigue, or confusion, and in this case can be reduced by 'stopping to think'.

Non-conscious mental activities demonstrably affect us even though they remain outside awareness. Solutions to problems, or creative ideas, may pop into our heads apparently without previous thought when, for example, particular memories or knowledge are activated by cues of which we are unaware, enabling us to see new ways forward: how to negotiate a deal or secure a broken window. More surprisingly, we can also make a decision to act without being aware of doing so. Olympic sprinters can take off in less than one-tenth of a second, before they can consciously perceive the sound of the starting gun, and changes in brain activity can be identified before people are aware of their intention to move.

Even more dramatic perhaps are the discoveries about 'blindsight'. After a surgical operation, a patient who was left partially blind claimed to be able to see nothing in a certain portion of his visual field. However, he was still able to tell whether a light presented to this part of his visual field was present or absent, and could distinguish above chance level between moving and stationary objects. Although he thought he was guessing, his 'guesses' reflected perception of which he remained unaware. Thus thinking is not, psychologically speaking, synonymous with conscious deliberation. It may only be useful for us to become aware of thinking when having to make a difficult choice (whether to change jobs), when events happen that cannot be handled automatically (the car breaks down leaving you stranded), or when unexpected feelings arise (someone makes you wildly angry).

The concepts with which we think are constructions that do not have to be precise and fixed so much as effective when we are thinking, reasoning, and communicating. It is often supposed that these activities are most successful when they conform to rules that we have learned, such as those of logic and grammar. However in practice their success has many other determinants.

Reasoning

Reasoning involves operating with the information we have in order to draw conclusions, solve problems, make judgements, and so on. Philosophers and logicians distinguish three types of reasoning which are useful for solving different kinds of problems: *deductive*, *inductive*, and *dialectical reasoning*. Although these provide the basis for our rationality, they are demonstrably influenced by psychological as well as logical processes.

Deductive reasoning follows formal rules, allowing us to draw conclusions which necessarily follow from the premisses on which they are based. From the two premisses 'if I am thinking then I am consciously using my brain', and 'I am thinking' we can validly draw the conclusion that 'I am consciously using my brain'. The conclusion may be false if either of the premisses is false, but the reasoning remains correct.

Psychologists studying deductive reasoning have found some typical errors, such as difficulty accepting unwelcome conclusions—that smoking causes cancer—or in changing valued beliefs, for example that all mothers are benign. We are especially bad at thinking about what is *not* the case, as is shown in Box 4.1.

Box 4.1. *Mistaken thinking*

Subjects were asked: Is the following argument valid?

Premisses: If it is raining, Fred gets wet.
It is not raining.
Conclusion: Fred does not get wet.

Over 30 per cent of subjects made errors. No valid conclusion can logically be drawn, as the premisses do not indicate what happens to Fred if it does not rain.

When a third premiss is added: 'If it is snowing, then Fred gets wet' the error rate decreases significantly.

Evans, 1989

Errors using deductive reasoning often occur when the truth or falsity of the premisses is unknown, and because our thinking is biased towards reinforcing our current beliefs and away from accepting information that contradicts them.

Indeed our thinking is subject to many illogical but useful biases. A friend of yours is sitting at home watching a football game. He tells you that if his team wins he will go to the pub. His team loses, and you 'reasonably', though not 'logically', go to find him at home (even though he has told you nothing about where he will be in these circumstances). Deductive reasoning alone would not lead you to this conclusion, but your 'irrationality' helps you meet up with your friend.

Inductive reasoning is the kind of reasoning upon which science mostly depends. Researchers make many careful observations and then draw conclusions that they think are probably true even though information yet to be discovered might show them to be false. It is commonly used in everyday life: 'Mary criticized what I said and dismissed my arguments out of hand'. 'Therefore Mary is a critical person.' Inductive reasoning allows us to come to conclusions that seem likely on the basis of our experience, and much of the time it works well. However, such probabilistic thinking can be wrong not only because unusual or rare events occur, but for many other reasons. One of the main ones is that we seek out information that confirms our conclusions (or suspicions) when we are in doubt, rather than going through the more logical, and informative, process of looking for information that would show we were wrong: in the example above for instance, that I had made many mistakes, rather than that Mary is always critical. As William James put it, 'a great many people think they are thinking when they are merely rearranging their prejudices'. Another problem is that we look for what we expect, and our expectations are affected by our feelings.

Reasoning is hard work, and often places a heavy load on memory. In practice we use many *heuristics*, or rules of thumb, to guide our thinking. Heuristics help us to solve complex problems. For example, the *availability heuristic* involves estimating the probability of a certain type of event on the basis of how easy it is to bring to mind relevant instances. The more readily available, the more likely it will seem to us to be. So the first thing I do when the printer does not work is to check whether I turned it on. My usual mistake springs readily to mind, and this simple action quickly solves the problem. So the heuristic brings with it problem-solving advantages that outweigh its disadvantages. The main disadvantage is that there are many determinants of availability—of what springs readily to mind—such as whether information has *recently* been thought about, is especially *vivid*, or is *emotionally charged*, and all of these factors may be logically irrelevant. So people who are frightened of flying tend to overestimate the likelihood of plane crashes, and to do so more dramatically if they have recently heard about a crash.

Dialectical reasoning is the ability to evaluate opposing points of view and to think critically so as to determine what is true or false or to resolve differences. It refers to the ability to use a range of reasoning skills when thinking, rather than to a type of logic or scientific method. Psychological difficulties with dialectical reasoning arise, for example, when it is important for someone to be right, or to have their beliefs accepted. Self-esteem can improve when people are right (or on the winning side) and fall when they are wrong (or on the losing side). Experience, feelings, and inclinations are amongst the many psychological factors that interfere with our ability to think with an open mind. In order to reason dialectically we need to absorb and remember much complex information, and to analyse issues dispassionately and critically. Our feelings and memories place measurable limits on our powers of reasoning. So does the 'packaging' of the messages we receive. For example, presenting political information on TV in 'sound-bites', shortened to be easily digestible and remembered, demonstrably interferes with critical thinking. Simplified ideas, presented to us in ways likely to divert or entertain, can be picked up even if watching TV mindlessly while doing something else. So thinking can be influenced by the way in which information reaches us, and psychological factors contribute much to the complexities involved in thinking and reasoning.

What we need now are good theories to explain and predict how human reasoning works, and why it is so hard to construct an adequate, artificial simulation of it. One of the most promising theoretical possibilities is that we form *mental models* representing what we know, and the validity or otherwise of conclusions based on the premisses we consider is assessed on the basis of those models. The processes of thinking and reasoning therefore depend upon the way in which we construct internal representations of concepts, and other thinking tools, such as images and propositions. Rather than standing or falling on the basis of their logicality, such processes succeed when they help us to operate in the world and fail when they do not.

Another approach to understanding how we use what gets into the mind is, therefore, to think in terms of the problems we have to solve. In most areas of life and much of the time, we are making judgements and decisions under conditions of uncertainty. We are thinking about what to do, or what will happen without knowing the answers. Will it rain? Can I afford a holiday? Will the children want to go swimming? How am I doing at work? At our disposal we have the ability to reason logically, and the ability to notice and avoid some of the most obvious sources of irrationality. We can behave as rational animals and we can also switch into automatic modes and behave mindlessly without putting our lives at risk (driving on the motorway while having an interesting conversation). In order to solve problems it helps to draw on internal representations, reasoning, and memory—and on all those 'reasonable' if not entirely rational cognitive abilities that help us to make decisions under conditions of uncertainty.

Problem solving has been studied by psychologists for about 100 years, and one of the topics in which they have been particularly interested is the way it is influenced by past experience—by information stored in memory. It sounds obvious that, in general, we solve problems more easily as we accumulate experience. This is known as the *positive transfer effect*, and it helps to explain why adults solve problems more easily than children, and experts solve them more easily than novices. Experts are better than novices at devising strategies for solving a chess problem for instance, but both novices and experts benefit from a period of *incubation* during which they are not (consciously) thinking about the problem at all. Once a strategy for solving a problem has been identified, it may take skill to apply the strategy (rescuing the curdled mayonnaise), and reasoning skills are needed to evaluate the progress being made. Experts are demonstrably better at recognizing patterns, retrieving relevant rules, and eliminating dead-end strategies. But experts can also fail to solve problems precisely because they use the same strategies and rules as they have used to solve previous problems. Developing a *mental set* prevents us having to reinvent the wheel each time we face a problem but slows us up when faced with a new set of difficulties. It is remarkable how blind experts can become.

Box 4.2. *Blinded by knowledge: mental set*

University students were presented with a problem which involved looking at a series of cards on which were written the letters A and B, and working out the 'correct' sequence (e.g. the letter on the left should be selected on the first card, and the letter on the right on the second card). After several 'position sequence' problems had been solved, the type of problem was changed so that selecting the letter A was always correct and the letter B was always incorrect. 80 per cent of the students failed to solve this, trivial, problem within 100 trials, and none of those who had failed to solve the problem selected the correct solution from amongst six possibilities.

Levine, 1971

Functional fixedness, or thinking about objects only in terms of their functions, is another kind of mental set that prevents problem solving. An envelope is something to put a letter into rather than a container for sugar when you are having a picnic. Solving the sugar problem requires thinking about envelopes in new and creative ways. Creativity has been measured in various ways: for example, by testing the degree to which people think *divergently*, and explore ideas freely, generating many solutions, or *convergently*, and follow a set of steps which appear to converge on one correct solution to a problem. The more uses they can think of for common objects such as a brick the more divergent or creative they are said to be.

We know that creativity is present at an early age: that young children can use familiar concepts in new and imaginative ways, and that environments that foster independent thinking in a safe way produce creative people. Creativity is not only important in the arts, but also in science, at home (especially in the kitchen), and in the office, and it may even confer adaptive advantages, by fostering an inventiveness which can be needed in constantly changing conditions. Creativity requires flexibility of thinking and an ability to step over boundaries (see Box 4.3), and, surprisingly to some people, it is only weakly correlated with intelligence. Characteristics such as nonconformity, confidence, curiosity, and persistence are at least as important as intelligence in determining creativity.

Box 4.3. *The 9-dot problem*

Task: using no more than four straight lines, and without lifting the pen from the paper, connect all the dots in the diagram below.

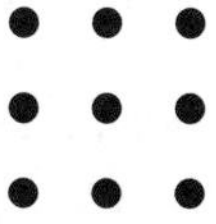

● ● ●

● ● ●

● ● ●

See pages 53–4 for solutions.

Communicating

Whenever we combine the representations we have in our head in new ways, to make something new, to solve problems, or to express ourselves, we are being creative, and one of the most obvious ways in which we do this is in our use of language. But how are language and thought related?

The *theory of linguistic relativity* suggests that language fosters habits of thinking and perception and that different languages therefore point speakers towards different views of reality. Linguistic evidence is fascinating. It shows us for instance that Eskimos have many different descriptions for snow, that the Chinese have no common word for orgasm, and that the French language is rich in food metaphors. And we know that snow is important to Eskimos, that the Chinese are reticent about discussing sexual matters, and the French renowned for their cooking. We also know that we can learn each others' languages and can learn to perceive or understand the distinctions made in languages other than our own. But linguistic and cultural information alone does not prove that language influences thought. The experiment in Box 4.4 demonstrates how the combination of clear thinking and accurate observations helps to provide an answer to such questions.

The evidence is accumulating to show that language can influence specific mental skills, but the jury is still out on the relationship between language and thought. Psychological as well as linguistic knowledge is needed to answer the question about whether language influences thinking, and scientifically watertight ways of investigating this question have not yet been devised.

Work on the cognitive skills involved in thinking, reasoning, and communicating is still expanding. It covers the acquisition and development of these abilities, problems arising with them, interactions between them, and much else besides. Perhaps the point to emphasize is that, in order to function well and adapt as we go, we need to achieve a balance between mindlessness and mindfulness—to know when to snap into action or stop and think. If we operated entirely on

---

Box 4.4. *Does language influence the acquisition of mental skills?*

Asian children are consistently better at mathematics than English-speaking children and in their languages the names for numbers reflect a base-10 system. The label for 12 is 'ten-two' and so on. Some children from three Asian and three Western countries in their first year at school were asked to stack blue blocks, representing 10 units, and white blocks representing 1 unit, into piles to show particular numbers. More Asian than Western children were able to make two correct constructions for each number. The Asian children used two blocks representing 10 units more than the Western children, and the Western children used the single-unit blocks more than the Asian children.

Conclusion: language differences may influence mathematical skills.

The evidence is strengthened by the finding that bilingual Asian-American children also score more highly on mathematical tests than do those who speak only English.

Miura and colleagues in 1994.

---

the basis of logic, like a robot or Mr Spock, we would be unable to adapt flexibly to the complexities and uncertainties of the everyday world. Hence there are still some respects in which our abilities appear superior to those of artificially intelligent machines, even though the machines may have larger memories and be able to test hypotheses faster than us. In particular, of course, we have feelings as well as thoughts, which may help us to understand why we do the things that we do.

Solution to 9-dot problem, Box 4.3

This problem can only be solved by continuing some of the lines outside the boundary of the square defined by the dots, or by breaking the 'boundary' in some other way: e.g. cutting the dots into three rows and arranging them in one continuous line.

References

Evans, J. St B. T. (1989). *Bias in Human Reasoning*. Hove, Erlbaum Ltd.

Levine, M. (1971). 'Hypothesis theory and non-learning despite ideal S-R reinforcement contingencies'. *Psychological Review*, 78: 130–40.

Miura, I. T., Okamoto, Y., Kim, C.-C., Chang, C.-M., *et al.* (1994). 'Comparisons of children's representation of number: China, France, Japan, Korea, Sweden and the United States'. *International Journal of Behavioral Development*, 17: 401–11.

5 Why do we do what we do? Motivation and Emotion

*F*eelings do not just give colour to our experience, or provide the emotional weather through which we travel. They serve a purpose. They provide an impetus to action, and we often explain our actions in terms of those things that we felt at the time: I thumped the table because I was angry, avoided speaking because I felt nervous, or found myself a drink because I felt thirsty. Motivations (hunger, thirst, sex) determine the goals towards which I strive, and emotions (happiness, frustration, despair) reflect the feelings I experience along the way. However, the two are often grouped together in psychology textbooks, and when not explained the juxtaposition can be mystifying. What have anger and thirst got in common, other than that you can 'feel' them? The main reason for treating them together is that they galvanize us into action. We talk about them as if they were forces within us, pushing us this way and that; forces that are felt in the body, which keep changing, and which may not always be understandable or logical. But they are not independent of other psychological factors. They both influence and are influenced by the processes described so far: perception, attention, learning, memory, thinking, reasoning, and communicating, and one of the problems for psychologists is to work out how these processes interact with feelings to explain why we do what we do.

Emotions organize our activities. They tell us what we want: to do well at work, a good meal, time out from all the hassle, and also what we do not want: another argument or increase in taxes. They bring with them a tendency to act in a particular way. Emotions can function as motives; a distressed or frightened child will seek comfort and security, or cry out for help, and (mostly) people seek to be close to those that they love. So logic is not enough. Imagine trying to decide what job to do, who to trust—or even marry—in the absence of feelings. All of the sophisticated mental equipment inside the human head has evolved so that when it functions well it helps us to get what we want and to avoid what we do not want. Motivations and emotions are the mobilizers of the otherwise purely mental machine—the fuel in the tank, and the way we behave, whether taking action or deciding not to do so, depends on the way in which feelings interact with the rest of the equipment.

Motivation: the pushes and prods

According to the Oxford English Dictionary motivation is 'the conscious or unconscious stimulus for action towards a desired goal provided by psychological or social factors; that which gives purpose or direction to behaviour'. Or, in psychological terms, as George Miller said: 'all those pushes and prods—biological, social and psychological—that defeat our laziness and move us, either eagerly or reluctantly, to action'. The motives behind our actions are guided by several forces: hunger is a biological motive, acceptance a social one, and curiosity a psychological one. So motivation is complex. Hunger, for example, is determined by external as well as internal factors—by the smell of newly cooked bread as well as by the emptiness of the stomach. If I am hungry I look for food, and the hungrier I am the harder I look and the longer I look for. Hunger determines the direction, intensity, and persistence of my behaviour—but it does not determine all aspects of my eating behaviour. I may also look for something to eat when I have an ache in my heart and not in my stomach, or just because that is my habit on entering the house.

Psychologists have categorized motives in illuminating ways. *Primary motives* help us to satisfy basic needs, such as those for food, drink, warmth, and shelter. These needs have to be satisfied to ensure survival, and they do not respond readily to attempts to control them voluntarily—one reason why it is so hard to diet. Some of them are cyclical (e.g. eating and sleeping) and the force with which they are felt increases and decreases in a more or less regular way. However, even these cyclical patterns are products of complex interactions—people who eat at regular times feel hungry if they miss a meal, whereas those who nibble all the time, or eat at irregular times, notice hunger pangs less.

Secondary motives (such as friendship or freedom—or 'honour, power, wealth, fame and the love of women' according to Freud) are acquired or learned, and the needs they satisfy may, or may not, be indirectly related to primary motives. Earning money enables me to satisfy a primary need for food and drink, but doing something creative like writing a story appears not to be related to a primary need. Some secondary motives are easily recognized: the need for friendship, or for independence, or being nice to someone out of guilt. Others may be outside conscious awareness, such as those things that I do to enhance or protect my self-esteem, or may be used as rationalizations for behaviour: avoiding conflict so as to keep others happy. In 1954 Maslow constructed a hierarchy ranging from lower level needs, satisfying which reduces deficiencies in physiological systems (needs for food and water), to higher level personal or abstract needs (Box 5.1).

Maslow believed that higher level needs will only emerge

Box 5.1. *Hierarchy of needs*

self-actualization and personal growth
aesthetic experience
cognitive activity
self-esteem
love and belonging
safety
survival

Maslow, 1954

when lower level needs are satisfied. The value of this theory has mainly been in the impetus it provided to the development of humanistic types of therapy. Many people in modern societies feel unhappy despite having their basic physiological needs met, which suggests that personal growth and the need to fulfil one's potential are important motivating forces, and more significant and profound motivators in humanistic terms, than lower level physiological forces: 'man cannot live by bread alone'. However, the theory has little empirical support, and self-actualization, which has no clear definition, may in practice depend upon external factors such as educational, cultural, and economic opportunities at least as much as it depends upon motivation.

There is as yet no adequate theory of motivation that accounts for all that is now known about lower level motives, such as physiological needs, and about higher level needs in which cognitive factors are important, such as the desire to be liked and accepted. However, it is clear, when it comes to understanding why we do what we do, that we need to encompass both types of need. Two contrasting theories illustrate the ways in which psychologists have thought about motivation: *homeostatic drive theory* and *goal theory*.

The basic idea in homeostatic drive theory is that it is important to maintain a reasonably constant internal environment. Any move away from this, or imbalance, prompts action to restore the balanced state. The action is 'driven' by the sense of imbalance, and continues until the balance is restored: the physiological effects of hunger send us to the kitchen, and eating what we find there reduces the disequilibrium, or discomfort, caused by the hunger. *Drive reduction theory* incorporated ideas about reinforcement into this basic homeostatic theory, suggesting that behaviours that successfully reduce a drive, like eating a chocolate when you are hungry, will be experienced as pleasurable and thus be reinforced. The motivation to continue the behaviour decreases as the drive is satisfied. We should therefore slow down, or stop eating when no longer hungry. What we actually do will depend on a combination of motivation (the hunger drive—or perhaps just the need for pleasure), and learning (about chocolates, where to find them and how many of them one can eat before feeling sick). The theory explains some aspects of complex behavioural patterns (refusing to eat so as to get attention) quite well. Satisfying the need for attention may help to re-establish a normal pattern of eating. However, the notion of drives does not apply to other aspects of behaviour such as tasting a new Mexican salsa, or eating the parsnips so as not to cause offence. Social, cognitive, and aesthetic factors motivate much of our behaviour, and these cannot be explained by drive-reduction theory without postulating a drive to match every contingency: a drive to listen to Schubert, and another for listening to Miles Davis, or walking along the top of the hill.

In contrast, *goal theory* attempts to explain why we do what we do in terms of cognitive factors, suggesting that the key to someone's motivation is what they are consciously trying to do: their goal. This theory suggests that people will work harder, and use more resources, when the goal is harder to achieve, and the harder the goal the higher the level of performance. An experiment testing this theory in the work-place is described in Box 5.2.

Box 5.2. *Doing your best*

Hypothesis: People given the hardest goal should perform best.

Method: Three sets of workers were given the task of cutting and transporting wood, working in small groups. The 'do your best' groups were given no goal, the 'assigned' groups were given a pre-assigned, hard goal, and 'participative' groups were required to set their own specific hard goal.

Results: The do your best group transported 46 cubic feet of wood an hour, compared with 53 cubic feet for the assigned group and 56 cubic feet for the participative group.

Latham and Yukl, 1975

Goal setting has been shown to improve performance in 90 per cent of the relevant studies, and it is especially likely to do so under the following conditions: people accept the goals set, they are informed about their progress, rewarded for achieving goals, have the ability to reach them, and are appropriately supported and encouraged by those in charge. These findings have been usefully applied in work settings, although we still need to know why some workers set higher goals than others, and how the motivating forces mobilized by setting one goal interact with others (physiological or social and so on).

Different motives therefore interact differently with physiological, cognitive, and behavioural systems, so that homeostatic drives play a central part in determining primary motives, and cognitive factors such as goals are more influential in determining secondary motives. For many of the things that we do a complex set of motives is involved. Research findings in this field have many practical applications, for example in helping us to motivate people to learn and to work, and helping us to understand and combat difficulties in motivational systems, such as those that result in obesity and the difficulties of dieting.

Emotion

It has been very difficult for psychologists to provide an adequate definition of emotion partly because measures of its components do not consistently correlate with each other. The five components psychologists distinguish are physiological (heart rate and blood pressure changes), expressive (smiling, frowning, slumping in a chair), behavioural (making a fist, running away), cognitive (perceiving a threat, danger, loss, or pleasure), and experiential (the complex of feelings experienced). I can smile when I am sad, and feel fearful without my heart rate changing, and this lack of correlation means that emotion cannot be properly studied and understood by measuring any one of its components.

Are there primary emotions, in the same way that there are primary colours? The issue is unsettled despite much cross-cultural and cross-species research, initiated by Charles Darwin. The facial expression of some emotions: for example fear, anger, sadness, surprise, disgust, and happiness, are sufficiently similar to be recognizable in people from different ethnic groups and also in many animals. However, possibly because of the lack of concordance between the five components of emotion, a much greater variety of emotions can be identified at the experiential than at the physiological or expressive levels, and of course there are as many types of smile and frown as there are people to express them and situations to provoke them. Complex emotions like guilt and shame, which are strongly determined by cognitive factors, such as what we think about ourselves, what we think others think, and internalized social rules, do not, so far as we yet

know, differ physiologically and are easy to confuse if one re-
lies solely on observable expressions.

Most of the time we experience mixtures of emotions, or
shades of feelings as various as the colours we perceive, rather
than pure states. Although there are common aspects of these
feelings, so that you and I can both feel sad, recognize it in
each other, and know what we mean when we talk about it,
my experience of sadness will differ from yours. The meaning
that it has for me, and the way in which I am able to express it,
is determined by the way in which it fits into my world right
now, by my past experience, memories, thoughts, reactions,
and the ways in which others have previously reacted to my
feelings of sadness. If they have told me to go away and stop
bothering them I may hide it or find it hard to talk about. The
point is that both the experience and the expression of emotions are products of complex processes which psychologists
are only now beginning to understand.

Different emotions appear to be governed by different parts
of the brain; anger and sadness predominantly involve the
right hemisphere while emotions such as happiness mostly
involve the left hemisphere. Even week-old babies respond to
different emotions differently in their two frontal lobes: a part
of the brain that is known to have special significance for
emotion. This could be because the two hemispheres are also
differentially specialized for the control of muscles with the
right hemisphere having better control over the large muscles
involved in fight or flight. Whether this specialization confers
other advantages is not known, but there is evidence that the
part of the brain called the *limbic system* functions as an emotional centre, and that layers of convoluted grey matter (*cortex* and *neocortex*) developed later in evolutionary terms,
thereby adding the ability to think about feelings, amongst
other things.

Information travels speedily and directly into and out of the
limbic system, only reaching centres of cognition later, thus

making us susceptible to 'emotional hijacking': the burst of anger or paroxysm of fear that overtake us despite our having decided to remain calm and in control of our sensibilities. In extreme fear we may react 'primitively' by jumping out of the way of the juggernaut, thus saving our lives, or more thoughtfully, by calling appropriate emergency services. A primitive reaction to hunger might involve eating all the chocolates available, like a bear that gorges on autumn fruit before the winter cold starts, and a more reasoned one involves 'holding back', or not 'giving in'. So strategic behaviours are needed to combat the pressure from more primitive systems, and these give rise to all manner of complex emotions ranging from self-satisfaction to unsatisfied longing.

Box 5.3. *The pivot of the internal self...*

'... the pivot of the internal self is emotion. This dominant "self-ish" brain lies in frontal lobe and limbic system linkages that appraise threats in the environment and organise quick actions. Human beings can override this usual mode of operation: actions can be reconsidered, we can learn and grow from experiences, conscious control can modify ineffective tendencies. But most often and most reliably, especially in eras long gone, feeling our way through worked best.'

from *The Evolution of Consciousness*; Ornstein, 1991: 153.

The evolutionarily primitive aspect of emotion helps to explain its power to disrupt thinking (see Box 5.3). When we are emotionally upset and complain that we can no longer think straight we are in fact quite correct. The frontal lobes play an important part in working memory, and they cannot function well when the limbic system (involved in emotion) is dominant and demands full attention. This observation focused the attention of psychologists on finding out how control over emotions is acquired, and it has many practical applications such as helping to change attitudes towards disruptive children who are slow to learn. Those who are distressed and disturbed will find it difficult to learn because of their high degree of emotional arousal, and their potential for school learning can be enhanced by alleviating their distress as much as (or more than) by increased teaching.

One of the most interesting unsolved problems in this field of psychology concerns the nature of the relationship between thoughts and feelings. Early theories of emotion focused primarily on the relationships between our experience of emotion and bodily changes, and on attempts to answer the chicken and egg type problem of which came first: the leap in the heart or the experience of the fear. These theories fail to explain how a particular perception is interpreted by the cognitive system: how we know that the situation we are in is dangerous, exciting, or safe.

Cognitive labelling theory (or *two factor theory*), developed in the early 1960s, stimulated a new approach to the study of emotion. According to this theory, emotional experience is determined by a combination of physiological arousal and the *labelling*, or interpretation, of the sensations experienced during that arousal. In order to test this theory ingenious experiments were devised that involved varying some components of emotion while holding others constant, as described in Box 5.4. The findings from these experiments have been taken to demonstrate the role of cognition in the experience of emotion. What we experience is greatly influenced by cognitive factors; by what we know about a situation, by how we interpret what happens to us internally and externally and of course by what we have learned and remembered about such situations in the past.

Despite flaws in the experiments done at this time, cognitive labelling theory had a major impact, and subsequent research into cognitive aspects of emotion has contributed much to the understanding of emotional distress and to the development of psychological treatments. Cognitive therapies, particularly for depression and anxiety, are based on the

Box 5.4. *Do I know what I feel?*

Aim: To find out what will happen when people have similar physiological symptoms of arousal but experience emotionally different situations.

Method: Some research subjects, supposedly participating in a test of the effects of a new vitamin on visual skills, were injected with adrenaline (which is physiologically arousing) and others were injected with a saline solution. Only some of those injected with adrenaline were correctly informed of its effects. While waiting for the drug to take effect the subjects were put in a situation designed to produce either euphoria or anger (using a stooge).

Results: After the waiting period the emotion the subjects reported reflected the mood expressed by the stooge, and was clearly influenced by social and cognitive factors. Those who had received the adrenaline injection but had not been correctly informed of its effects were most emotional. They were most likely to report feeling relatively happy or irritable later according to how the stooge had behaved. Those subjects who had been correctly informed responded less strongly to the behaviour of the stooge and appeared to attribute their experience at least partly to the injection.

Conclusion: Our awareness of the situation we are in influences the emotion that we actually feel, but our physiological state *determines how strongly we feel it.*

Schachter and Singer, 1962

idea that thoughts and feelings are so intimately related that changing one will change the other. As it is difficult to change feelings directly, cognitive therapies attempt to change them indirectly by working in therapy to change thinking, finding new ways of seeing things or developing new perspectives. For example, the loss of a relationship may be interpreted as meaning that I will never find another partner (a thought which makes me sad, and which makes it hard for me to get out and about to meet more people), but could also be interpreted as meaning that, although I am understandably upset, I still have the characteristics that my lost partner found attractive, and can still make new friends. In other words, understanding more about the cognitive aspects of emotion has helped us to understand more of the intricacies of the relationships between thoughts, feelings, and behaviour in general. In turn, this has guided the development of cognitive therapies which are demonstrably effective in helping people who are experiencing a wide range of emotional difficulties.

For many years experimental psychologists paid little systematic attention to feelings, making the assumption that useful explanations of human behaviour were more likely to be found elsewhere. Indeed, we do tend to assume that feelings get in the way, or that they interfere with otherwise rational behaviour, and some psychologists seem to have assumed that feelings were more properly the province of clinicians, whose understanding of feelings is informed by personal qualities such as sensitivity and the ability to empathize as well as by their knowledge of the more scientific aspects of psychology. This view, however, gives insufficient weight to the evolutionary functions of motivation and emotion.

Fear organizes us for flight; anger for attack. Of course, feelings such as anger can get us into trouble as well as out of trouble, but without them we might put ourselves at risk, and we also depend on them for defining goals and organizing ourselves to work towards them. It has even been argued that there is such a thing as emotional intelligence—a quality that varies between people, that can be more or less successfully employed to help us achieve our aims, and which psychologists should study carefully so as to discover how to assist in its acquisition, development, or increasing sophistication.

The study of motivation and emotion has contributed to clinical fields as widely different as those of psychoanalysis, humanistic and cognitive therapies, and the development of programmes for those who need help with primary needs such as eating, drinking, and sex and with secondary needs such as smoking and gambling. It has been able to do so because, in order to study feelings and to answer questions about why we do what we do, it has proved necessary to think in terms of many interacting systems: physical, cognitive, affective, behavioural, and socio-cultural. The complexity of doing this means that there is still much to learn. Our increased understanding of the interactions between emotional arousal and the capacity to attend, learn, and remember has had some practical uses. For example, we have stopped using lie detectors, which only measure one component of emotion and cannot therefore be reliable. The complexity of the field may explain why there is still debate about such important issues as the effects of watching scenes of violence on television, and the question of whether it is better to bottle up anger or to express it.

References

Latham, G. P., and Yukl, G. A. (1975). 'Assigned versus participative goal setting with educated and uneducated woods workers'. *Journal of Applied Psychology*, 60: 299–302.

Maslow, A. H. (1954). *Motivation and Personality.* New York, Harper.

Miller, G. (1967). *Psychology: The Science of Mental Life*. London, Penguin Books.

Ornstein, R. (1991). *The Evolution of Consciousness: The Origins of the Way We Think.* New York, Touchstone.

Schachter, S., and Singer, J. R. (1962). 'Cognitive, social and physiological determinants of emotional state'. *Psychological Review*, 69: 379–99.

6 Is there a set pattern?
Developmental Psychology

*T*he most obvious way in which people develop is physical: transforming them from tiny, helpless babies into more or less capable adults. However, development, and especially psychological development, does not end when physical maturity is reached—it continues throughout adulthood. The findings of developmental psychologists reveal what is developmentally typical and this has many practical uses in advising parents about what to expect at different ages, planning education programmes, determining when a child is not developing normally, predicting the effects of early experience on later behaviour, and creating appropriate opportunities for older people.

Developmental psychology is concerned both with mapping the changes that occur with age and with understanding how those changes take place—the *process* of development. Two questions are particularly important in looking at processes. First, does development take place in stages or is the process more continuous than that? And second, is development biologically determined by 'nature' (the genetically programmed process of physical maturation) or influenced by environmental circumstances (by 'nurture')? The concept of stages suggests that everyone passes through the same stages in the same order, reaching the later ones only by going through the earlier. It clearly is necessary to acquire basic before complex skills: to learn to count before learning to add, or to grasp before lifting, and rough stages of development are reflected in the terms 'baby', 'child', and 'adult'. But are there also finer stages? If so, how flexible are they? Observation suggests that development is not as fixed as the idea of stages suggests: most children crawl before they can walk, but some do not.

Exceptions to the rule led developmental psychologists to propose that there are *critical periods* in human development—that is, time periods during which events must occur for development to proceed normally. For example, if a human foetus does not receive the correct hormones before the seventh week, a genetic male may fail to develop male sexual organs until puberty triggers another bout of hormonal activity. There is some evidence that there are also critical, or at least sensitive, periods in psychological development. Case studies such as the one in Box 6.1 suggest that children who have not started to learn language by about the age of 7, find it very difficult to learn later.

Genie's case is an extreme example of how environmental circumstances can affect development. The relative

---

Box 6.1. *A case of extreme deprivation: Genie*

Genie came to the attention of the authorities when she was 13. She had been treated extremely harshly by her parents—she spent nearly all the time alone and tightly bound. She was never spoken to and was beaten for making any sound. When she was discovered, Genie lacked many basic skills—she could neither chew nor walk upright, was incontinent, and understood little language. Genie was given intensive rehabilitation and eventually placed in a foster home. She made amazing progress in developing both physical and social skills. However, although she learnt to understand and use basic language, her grammar and pronunciation remained abnormal.

importance of genetic and environmental factors—the nature/nurture question—arises in many topics in psychology, but is of special relevance when thinking about development. Observations of extraordinary similarities between twins reared apart, for example in their preferences for certain styles of dress or music, suggest that predetermined pathways may not be modifiable during the course of development. However, more thorough work has now convinced most psychologists that components of both 'nature' and 'nurture' are required for healthy development. For example, the potential to learn a spoken language is inborn (nature component), but the rate of language learning, the form of the language, accent, vocabulary, and ability to use it to express complex thoughts or feelings, is determined by 'nurture', including cultural influences such as those affecting the different ways in which men and women use language.

What is inborn?

As already mentioned in Chapter 3, babies are born predisposed to learn. They are born with useful reflexes such as sucking and grasping, and babies only a few days old can discriminate voices and prefer looking at faces. At one month babies can discriminate sounds in order to gain a sweet taste. In all species, the young appear to be primed to learn skills that are useful—and human babies may be 'set up' with abilities that encourage care-giving from adults. For example, newborn babies cannot adapt the focus of their eyes as objects move closer and farther away, but focus at approximately the distance at which they are typically held. Similarly, newborn babies' exceptional ability to discriminate speech sounds allows them to recognize and show a preference for their mother's voice by the time they are three days old. It is even possible that some learning takes place in the womb—newborn babies respond differently to their mother's language than to other languages. However, an 'innate' potential (or ability) may guide and facilitate subsequent learning. The experiment in Box 6.2 suggests that babies are born able to organize and interpret the flood of sensory stimuli they experience, as if they were already using some elementary perceptual principles (such as those described in Chapter 2).

Box 6.2. *What do babies know about numbers?*

Babies 6–8 months old were shown a series of pairs of slides, one showing three and the other showing two objects. At the same time as seeing a pair of slides the baby heard either two or three drumbeats from a central speaker. The babies tended to look longer at the slide that matched the number of drumbeats. So when there were two drumbeats the babies spent more time looking at the slide with two objects. These results suggest that babies can abstract numerical information sufficiently well to recognize similarity or to 'match' like with like. It is not suggested that they have specific knowledge about numbers, but that they have some innate ability that helps them to learn about them.

The child's development

More changes occur in the first few years of life than in any other time period. For example, you grow half your height and learn enough language to communicate basic needs by the age of 2. Although no formal training is required for children to learn basic skills such as walking and talking, there is much variation in the rate at which children learn these skills. Developmental psychologists have tried to find out what factors influence this process. Children who are raised in institutions where they get little attention or few opportunities to play develop at a slower rate than children in more stimulating environments. However, the detrimental effects of understimulation can be remedied by the opportunity to play for as little as one hour a day.

Observations of children raised in deprived environments suggest that when opportunities for exercise and movement are impoverished, there is some delay in both cognitive and motor development: as if playing helped a child to think. Such findings led developmental psychologists to question whether extra stimulation or training accelerated the development of children who were not deprived. This idea was tested by experiments like the one in Box 6.3.

Box 6.3. *Does extra practice help babies develop?*

One of a pair of identical twins was given a lot of early practice at a particular skill, such as crawling. Later, the other twin was given a brief period of practice and the performance of both twins was compared. In general, the twins performed about the same if the least practised one had had even a little practice. For basic motor skills, a little practice later (when the child is physically more mature) can be as good as a lot of practice earlier.

Personality and social development

If physical development is governed by experience as well as by the process of physical maturation, is this also true for other aspects of development such as personality and social development? Babies develop social responses very early indeed: 2-month-old babies of different cultures, and even blind babies, smile at their mothers—an action that is likely to strengthen the mother–child bond. The universality of smiling suggests that maturation is important in determining its onset. By 3 or 4 months babies recognize and prefer familiar people, but they remain friendly towards strangers until about 8–12 months old when a fear of strangers develops. Both distress on separation and fear of strangers decrease by the age of 2 or 3 when children are more able to take care of some of their own needs. These changes make evolutionary sense: the fear of strangers increases with mobility and then decreases with increasing capability.

It has been suggested that the child's bond with its *primary care-giver* (the person who does the majority of the caring for the child) is crucial in determining later psychological development. For example, in 1951 John Bowlby maintained that 'mother love in infancy and childhood is as important for mental health as are vitamins and proteins for physical health'. More recently, he has suggested that people with psychiatric disorders tend to show the kind of disturbance in their social relationships that could result from poor bonding in childhood. Developmental psychologists have investigated whether the quality and/or quantity of early relationships does indeed determine later functioning, and what factors influence early relationships.

A child's early relationships are often referred to as *attachments*—that is, relatively enduring emotional ties to a particular person (the *attachment figure*). Attachment can be measured by how much babies and young children seek to be near the attachment figure, and are generally oriented towards them, becoming upset when they leave and happy when they return. Attachments may enable children to feel secure in new settings, so they can explore both physically and psychologically, gradually increasing their independence and *detachment* from the attachment figure. Attachment normally peaks between 12 and 18 months and gradually declines after that, but its effects may persist.

Table 6.1 describes how developmental psychologists have classified the quality of children's attachments by observing their behaviour in a structured setting, called the *strange situation*, in which a child and its mother are in a room full of toys. After some time they are joined by someone who is a stranger to the child, then the mother leaves and returns a short while later. The child's behaviour is observed at all stages through a one-way mirror.

TABLE 6.1. *Types of attachment*

General description	Response to mother leaving	Response to mother returning	Response to stranger
Anxious-avoidant	Largely unaffected by mother's presence —pay little attention to her and do not appear distressed by her leaving.	Usually, these babies make little effort to contact mother on her return.	Usually are not distressed by stranger's presence. Generally treat mother and stranger in a similar manner, e.g. are as easily comforted by stranger as by mother.
Securely attached	As long as mother is present, they play happily. They are clearly upset when she leaves.	Immediately seek and gain comfort from mother, then resume play.	Friendly to strangers when mother is present, but are distressed in her absence. Clearly more attached to mother than to stranger.
Anxious-resistant	Have difficulty in using mother as a safe base for exploration, tend to become upset when she is not at hand, and very upset when she leaves.	Seem ambivalent towards mother when she returns, e.g. cry to be picked up then scream to be put down.	They resist the efforts of the stranger to make contact.

Although initially it was thought that babies were showing 'cupboard love'—that they became attached to their mothers primarily because they were the main source of food, experiments with monkeys such as the one in Box 6.4 suggest that this is not the case.

In humans, it seems that the most important factors influencing attachment are the child's temperament (its 'nature') and the attachment figure's *responsiveness*—understanding of and sensitivity to the child's needs. The attachment figures of insecurely attached babies tend to re-

Box 6.4. *Attachment in monkeys*

Infant monkeys were separated from their mothers shortly after birth and were given two substitute 'mothers'. Both substitute mothers were made from wire mesh with wooden heads. One was covered with foam padding and terry-cloth, making it more 'cuddly'. The other was bare wire but dispensed milk from a bottle attached to its chest. The monkeys showed much more attachment to the 'cuddly' mother in spite of the fact that it was the other mother that gave them milk.

spond more on the basis of their own needs than to the baby's signals. For example, playing with the baby when it is convenient for them rather than when the baby shows signs of wanting to play. This may explain why a child's strongest attachment may not be to the person who does most of the physical caretaking. It seems that the quality of care is more important than the quantity in determining a child's attachments.

Effects of early experience

An important enterprise for developmental psychology has been to try to determine whether early experiences such as poor parenting affect later development, and if the effects of a deprived early life can be ameliorated. The experiments in Box 6.5 investigate this issue.

Although it would be unethical to carry out such experiments with human babies, case studies such as that of Genie (described in Box 6.1) give some information about the effects of early derivation, and Box 6.6 describes a study which investigated how separation affects later development.

In general, studies suggest that infants who are securely attached are better equipped to cope with new experiences and relationships, and research is accumulating to suggest that

Box 6.5. *Investigating the effects of early deprivation*

Raising monkeys in total or partial isolation (where they can see but not touch other monkeys) has shown that such conditions lead to highly maladaptive behaviour—these monkeys were socially withdrawn and aggressive to their peers, they had difficulty mating, and often subsequently became abusive mothers. However, if the monkeys were reintegrated by three months, or if they were given even one playmate, they could develop normally. Other experiments involved raising monkeys with 'abusive mothers'—which were cloth monkeys that blasted the infants with cold air. These studies found that the 'abused' baby monkeys showed stronger attachments to their 'mothers'.

Box 6.6. *The effects of separating babies from their parents*

In one study of children who had been placed in care by the age of 4 months, it was found that those who had been adopted by the age of 4 years subsequently developed much better than those who had been returned to their natural parents, or those who remained in the institution. This may have been due to the higher social class of the adoptive parents, or because the 'returned' children went back to homes that still had many problems. These results show that the detrimental effects of early separation can be ameliorated, and that attachments formed as late as 4 years old can provide a basis for healthy development. Moreover, the finding that some of the children who remained in the institution were doing better than those returned to their natural parents contradicts Bowlby's view that 'mother love' is always best.

poor attachment in infancy could be an early precursor on the developmental pathway to later psychopathology. Such research findings can provide a sound scientific grounding for clinical theories, and may contribute to the development of better ways of relieving some clinical problems and helping parents to be better care-givers. Moreover, many studies show that the harmful effects of early experiences can be ameliorated, particularly if the child is still young when the conditions are improved. In fact, many researchers have been struck by children's resilience in that there is a tendency towards normal development under all but the most adverse circumstances.

Development over the lifespan

People continue to develop both physically and psychologically throughout their lives. Whilst changes such as puberty are at least partly due to physical maturation, others reflect a substantial degree of environmental influence. For instance, people tend to adopt a more sedentary lifestyle with increasing age but this may simply be a reaction to environmental changes such as retirement and decreasing social involvement and physical health. In 1968 Erikson proposed a stage theory of lifespan development which suggests that human development follows the pattern set out in Table 6.2.

This theory suggests that there are definite stages, each involving a specific task or *psychosocial crisis*, that everyone progresses through during a lifetime. For example, the main task of adolescence is seen as being a search for identity. Initially, largely on the basis of observations of adolescents referred for treatment, adolescence was seen as a turbulent period characterized by rebellion and rejection of authority figures. However, studying the general population of adolescents revealed that many do not rebel against authority but maintain good relationships with parents and teachers throughout. This is one example demonstrating the pitfalls which arise when observations are taken from a small and unrepresentative sample of the larger population. Subsequent studies investigating adolescents from all backgrounds have been more struck by the amount of *role transition* during this period. During adolescence many new roles such as that of worker or boyfriend/girlfriend, and adult-to-adult interaction

TABLE 6.2. *Stages of development*

Stages	Psycho-social crises	Primary activity	Significant relation-ships	Favourable outcome
First year	Trust vs. mistrust	Consistent stable care	Main care-giver	Trust and optimism
2 to 3	Autonomy vs. doubt	Independence from parents	Parents	Sense of autonomy and self-esteem
4 to 5	Initiative vs. guilt	Environmental exploration	Basic family	Self-direction and purpose
6 to puberty	Industry vs. inferiority	Knowledge acquisition	Family, neighbours, and school	Sense of competence and achievement
Adolescence	Identity vs. confusion	Coherent vocation and personality	Peers, in- and out-groups	Integrated self-image
Early adulthood	Intimacy vs. isolation	Deep and lasting relationships	Friends and lovers; competition and cooperation	Ability to experience love and commitment
Middle adulthood	Generativity vs. self-absorption	Productive and creative for society	Divided labour and shared household	Concern for family, society and future generations
Late adulthood	Integrity vs. despair	Life review and evaluation	Mankind, extended family	Sense of satisfaction; acceptance of death

patterns are acquired. Erikson suggests that the most important task during adolescence is the process of coming to terms with these new roles: finding a single, integrated identity, in spite of having to act differently in many new roles. As each stage lays the foundation for the next one, this coherent sense of identity is thought to lay the foundation for later relationships and productivity in adulthood. Without an integrated identity, Erikson thought that people would experience *identity diffusion* and would have difficulty forming relationships, planning for the future, and achieving their goals. Without a clear sense of who we are, deciding what we want from the future is difficult.

Studies of declining cognitive functioning with increasing age also demonstrate the pitfalls of looking at subsamples of the population. Studies comparing intelligence test scores in groups of older and younger people showed that younger people had higher IQs, suggesting that intelligence declined with age. However, these studies failed to take account of the *cohort effect*—social determinants of performance on IQ tests and the fact that intelligence scores of the whole population had increased with better education and nutrition. When intelligence was measured repeatedly in the same people there was no evidence that it declined with age; rather, it increased slightly for those who continued to use their minds. Similarly, the supposed deterioration of memory with age does not stand up well to scientific investigation but suggests that the system responds to the demands you make of it. Comparisons of memory for everyday events show that older people perform slightly better than younger ones, possibly because they are more concerned about their memories and are more attentive and motivated during testing. The myth of declining memory with increasing age appears to be partly due to a self-fulfilling prophecy: because people expect to become more forgetful they try less hard and notice forgetting more than remembering. It appears that as long as people continue to keep their minds active, they need not expect a noticeable decline in their mental abilities until very late in life (in the absence of medical conditions such as dementia).

Although there is little scientific basis for the myth of declining intellect with age, there are some changes in behaviour that are typically associated with ageing. For example, in Western societies older people tend to be much less prominent than other age groups. *Disengagement theory* proposes that, as people age, a biological mechanism is activated and encourages them to gradually withdraw from society, just as an animal creeps away to die once its evolutionary function (ensuring the survival of its offspring) has been fulfilled. However, the analogy is a poor fit because in humans this process of disengagement does not tie in with the end of child-rearing, nor is it associated with poor physical health. In contrast, *activity theory* explains the disengagement of older people as a societal process: there are fewer roles for older people to play in society, and retirement may reduce opportunities to play a valuable part in everyday living. Although some people replace their working roles with other valuable activities, others do not, and may feel useless or isolated. The effects of changes in activity associated with ageing may be exacerbated in Western societies by 'ageism'. Stereotypes of older people are generally negative—that they are less intelligent, sickly, lazy, rigid in their views, and bad-tempered. As with other forms of prejudice such stereotypes are largely false—for example, it is the exception rather than the rule for older people to become confused. Like other prejudices, ageism can be self-maintaining in that positive contributions made by older people are overlooked while negative factors are remembered (see Chapter 9 for a fuller description of prejudices and how they can be overcome).

We have seen that many biological, social, and environmental factors influence developmental processes. Although there is a rough pattern for development, and self-righting tendencies stimulate constant adaptation, there are also many potential pitfalls. Because development is such a complex process, we should be cautious in interpreting differences between different age groups as such differences could result from changes over the generations, rather than from ageing itself. Nevertheless developmental psychology can indicate which factors affect development adversely and which do not, in fields as diverse as moral development, language acquisition, and the development of thinking and gender identity. Future challenges for developmental psychologists focus on finding ways of ameliorating the effects of negative early experiences, finding remedies for when development is not proceeding normally, and looking at ways of enhancing adjustment throughout the lifespan.

References

Bowlby, J. (1951). *Maternal Care and Mental Health*. World Health Organization Monograph Series No. 2. Geneva, World Health Organization; repr. (1966) New York, Schocken Books.
Erikson, E. H. (1968). *Identity, Youth and Crisis*. New York, Norton.

7 Can we categorize people? Individual Differences

*W*hile the previous chapter looked at typical developmental processes and patterns, emphasizing the similarities between people, this chapter is concerned with differences between people. Most of us prefer to think of ourselves as unique individuals, but is it possible to categorize the differences between us, and is it possible to identify the determinants of such differences? On the practical side, psychologists have developed ways of measuring people so as to find out more about the similarities and differences between them. These psychological assessments often take the form of paper and pencil measures such as aptitude or achievement tests, which are used to measure abilities or accomplishments, or to assess suitability for particular educational or occupational positions.

Psychological measurement

Psychological tests or *psychometric instruments* need to be both *reliable* and *valid*—that is, they should consistently measure the variable that they claim to measure. For example, a test of reading ability would not be considered a good test if it gave the same person very different scores when tested a few days apart (low reliability). Similarly, the test would lack validity if a person who could not read well scored highly on it. In order to be useful, psychological tests must also be *standardized*, which means that there must be an established set of 'norms' against which to compare individual scores. Standardizing tests involves giving the test to a large group of the type of people it is intended for, and using statistics to calculate *norms*—to work out what is an average score, and what proportion of the population score different amounts above or below this average. These norms can then be used to interpret an individual's test score. For instance, IQ tests are the best-known example of a psychometric test, and they are designed so that the population's average score is 100, and that 95 per cent of the population score between 70 and 130, so someone scoring 132 can be judged to be well above average (in the top 2.5 per cent). Psychologists have also found that the way in which a test is administered and the conditions of testing can influence the results. If the lighting is poor, or the person does not hear or understand the instructions, then their score may be artificially low. Thus, the conditions under which the test is administered must also be standardized— the test must be given to each person in exactly the same way, under similar conditions, if the results are to be valid.

Psychometric tests are used to assess a wide variety of abilities and attributes and this chapter will focus on the two facets of individual differences that have been most intensively studied and measured—intelligence and personality. As in other areas of psychology, there has been much debate about whether individual differences in intelligence and personality result from inheritance or from environmental influences (nature or nurture).

Intelligence

Despite being one of the most important concepts in psychology, intelligence is one of the most elusive to define.

Intelligence can simply be viewed as the ability to respond adaptively to one's environment, but this ability to respond adaptively may involve many aspects—such as being able to think logically, rationally, and abstractly, as well as the ability to learn and to apply this learning in new situations. Psychologists have questioned whether intelligence is a common thread underlying all mental processes or whether it reflects several different factors or types of intelligence. The abilities of *idiot savants*—people with low IQs but one extraordinary ability, such as being able to name the day of the week of any date in the last ten years—suggest that an individual can have vastly different abilities in different areas. Furthermore, a question of great practical interest has been whether intelligence is predetermined (inborn), or whether it can be learnt or enhanced in any way.

Intelligence tests

One of the simplest definitions of intelligence is to define it as 'what IQ tests measure'—a circular definition that raises issues concerning the relationship between IQ tests and definitions of intelligence. The way in which intelligence is defined influences the tests that are designed to measure it. For example, a *two-factor model* supposes that intelligence is made up of a general factor and specific factors, whereas other models suggest that there are a number of independent specific factors such as numerical reasoning, memory, musical ability, word fluency, visuo-spatial ability, perceptual speed, insight into oneself, and understanding of others, but no single general factor. Another approach has been to examine the processes involved in intelligence, such as the speed of processing, how information is represented internally, or the strategies used to solve problems.

Disagreements concerning definitions of intelligence lead to difficulties in constructing tools to measure it: any intelligence test is based on a particular definition or conceptualization of intelligence and thus may reflect the biases of the investigator. For example, timed tests place more emphasis on the speed of processing, whereas other tests may be designed to measure separate 'specific factors' or an innate general ability. Box 7.1 gives some examples of the items used in intelligence tests.

Box 7.1. *What intelligence tests ask*

Most intelligence tests contain several subscales, consisting of different types of questions. Some may simply ask for information with questions such as 'how many months are there in a year?' or 'what is the capital of Australia?' Other subscales may assess the person's digit-span by asking them to repeat increasingly long strings of numbers forwards or backwards, or assess their arithmetic by asking questions like 'raffle tickets cost 76 pence each, if I bought six tickets how much change would I get from £10?' Vocabulary or comprehension may be assessed by asking for definitions of common words, or by asking what the similarity is between word pairs such as 'orange-banana' or 'reward-punishment' (you would need to say that they were both a means of influencing the behaviour of others to get the maximum points). Other subscales may involve arranging pictures in the best order so they tell a story, or may be more practical such as arranging blocks to copy a design or doing jigsaw-like puzzles.

Intelligence tests usually give a score expressed as an *intelligence quotient* or IQ. As mental ability increases during the first eighteen years of life, the 'raw' test scores must be adjusted in the light of the person's chronological age. This is done with reference to norms for the person's age group. For children, scores are sometimes expressed as a *mental age*. Thus a particularly bright 7-year-old child, who performs as well as the average 10-year-old, could be said to have a chronological age of 7 but a mental age of 10.

Although they are widely used, intelligence tests have been criticized on many grounds. A fundamental difficulty is that they do not measure intelligence itself, but attempt to measure the qualities that are thought to reflect it. They have been validated primarily in terms of educational achievement, which may be less of a product of intelligence and more a product of other factors such as social class, opportunity, and motivation. Furthermore, intelligence tests are based on the idea that intelligence is an accurately measurable quantity, unaffected by temporary factors such as the situation, the person's state of mind, motivation, or recent experience. In fact, IQ scores are affected by temporary situational factors, and furthermore, they can be increased by practice at doing IQ tests.

A particularly controversial result of intelligence testing has been the finding that black Americans score significantly lower than white Americans on standard intelligence tests. In fact, most ethnic groups score lower than white middle-class groups on IQ tests. This finding has been interpreted by some as 'evidence' that some races are intellectually inferior, but other results, such as the finding that German babies fathered by black and white American soldiers have similar IQs, show that the difference between blacks' and whites' IQ scores is not due to genetic inferiority of blacks. It is much more likely that it reflects a deficit in standard IQ tests—they are biased in favour of white middle-class cultures. Questions such as being asked who led the country during a certain war may be biased towards those who have been educated in Western societies, who had relatives living in the country during that period, and who have a good command of the English language. There have been attempts to construct 'culture-fair' tests, which do not ask for culturally biased information and may not use language at all (see Box 7.2 for an example). However, it has proved almost impossible to be fair to more than one culture at a time. Furthermore, if intelligence is defined as the ability to respond adaptively to one's environment, some would argue that a bias towards white middle-class cultures is a realistic bias, given the current domination of these cultures in many societies.

Box 7.2. *'Culture-fair' intelligence test questions*

The subject is asked to choose which of the four items on the right best fits the pattern on the left.

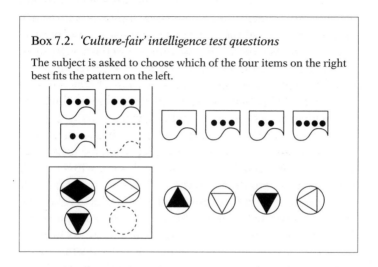

One suggestion that reconciles some of the disagreement about what intelligence is, and whether it is inborn, is the view that there are two basic types of intelligence: one that reflects a genetic potential or an inborn basic ability, and another that is acquired or learnt as experience interacts with potential. In 1963 Cattell suggested that 'fluid' intelligence is the inborn ability to solve abstract problems, whereas 'crystallized' intelligence involves practical problem solving and knowledge, which comes from experience.

Is intelligence influenced by the environment?

Psychologists often attempt to find out if something is determined by the environment or by genetics through studying identical twins (who are genetically identical) who have been brought up in different environments, or by looking at the similarity in intelligence between family members who are more or less closely related. The evidence from these studies supports both cases. For example, the similarity in intelligence between identical twins brought up together is much greater than that of those who have been separated early in life, suggesting a role for the environment in the development of intelligence. Furthermore, studies of adopted children show that their IQs are more similar to those of their adoptive than biological parents. However, there is greater similarity of intelligence between identical twins than between fraternal twins, suggesting a role for genetics! So both genetics and environmental factors exert an influence on intelligence, and it may not be possible—or even useful—to try to work out which is most important. Moreover, it is not always possible to separate genetic from environmental influences: for instance, a separated twin or adopted child may intentionally be placed in an environment that is similar to its original home, or the environment may influence the way in which a genetic potential is realized, as when mothers with lower socio-economic status receive poorer prenatal care, and have smaller babies.

Can intelligence be increased?

A question that is of greater practical use is whether intelligence can be enhanced by environmental influences. Even minimal interventions such as giving dietary or vitamin supplements have been shown to increase children's IQs by as much as 7 points, possibly through their effect on general health and thus, on factors such as energy, concentration, and attention. There is also evidence showing that the amount of parental attention a child receives affects its IQ—this may explain why there is a significant correlation between birth order and IQ, because the first child usually gets more attention, which may enhance IQ. Studies such as the one described in Box 7.3 suggest that educational interventions may also have an effect on later attainment.

Box 7.3. *Headstart project*

The headstart project was intended to compensate American preschool children for the effects of a disadvantaged environment. Day-care centres were set up to provide these children with extra stimulation and education, and their cognitive and social functioning was compared, over several years, with that of children who had not attended day-care centres. Although the initial results were discouraging, suggesting that any advantage for the 'headstart' group was short-lived, later reports found that there was a 'sleeper effect'—the headstart group scored higher on ability tests and this advantage increased as they got older. On a practical level, the children in the headstart group were less likely to be in a remedial class or to repeat a year at school, and were more likely to want to succeed academically. There was also an effect on the parents—the mothers of the 'headstart' children reported more satisfaction with their children's school work and had higher occupational expectations for their children.

Similarly, other studies have found that day-care interventions can increase IQ and so can the type of school. In one study children who went to more academic schools showed an average increase of 5 IQ points whereas those who went to less academic schools showed, on average, a decrease of 1.9 points.

What can be concluded from these studies on intelligence and IQ? First, there has yet to be agreement on a definition or model of intelligence. While we all have a general idea of what intelligence is, we use the term to describe many different things and this may be because it does in fact have a number of aspects which are more or less closely related to each other. The difficulties in agreeing a definition of intelligence are reflected in the tests that are used to measure it, and hence they do not always appear to be fair measures (e.g. they are biased towards white middle-class cultures). It seems likely that intelligence is too complex and poorly defined a construct to be reflected by a single number such as IQ. On the practical side, studies of intelligence have shown that while IQ is determined by both genetic and environmental influences, it is possible to manipulate environmental circumstances to produce enduring benefits, both in terms of IQ and achievement.

Personality

As a concept, personality is possibly even more central in psychology, and even more difficult to define than intelligence. Loosely speaking, personality reflects a characteristic set of behaviours, attitudes, interests, motives, and feelings about the world. It includes the way in which people relate to others and is thought to be relatively stable throughout life. One of the motivations behind psychologists' efforts to identify and measure the ways in which people's personalities differ is to be able to predict their future behaviour, so as to anticipate, modify, or control such behaviour. However, measuring personality suffers from similar difficulties as those inherent in measuring intelligence because, like intelligence, it cannot be measured directly—it can only be inferred from the behaviours that are thought to reflect it.

Several theories of personality have been proposed and the main approaches are summarized in Table 7.1.

Each of the different approaches in Table 7.1 reflects a comprehensive theory and it is not possible to cover any of them in depth here. Instead we will highlight some of the main ways in which they differ and use Eysenck's (1965) theory of personality, which combines elements of both the type and trait approaches, as an example.

Different theories of personality vary in the degree to which they see behaviours as determined by people or by the situa-

TABLE 7.1.

Approach	View of personality
Categorical type	People are fitted into broad categories, with each type being qualitatively different from others e.g. type A or B; introvert or extrovert.
Trait	A descriptive approach in which people are defined according to how much of each of a list of traits they have, e.g. high conscientiousness, low introversion.
Behaviourist	Views personality as merely a reflection of the person's learning history—they simply repeat the responses that have been reinforced in the past.
Cognitive	Sees beliefs, thoughts, and mental processes as primary in determining behaviour across situations.
Psychodynamic	Based on Freud's work and sees personality as determined by intrapsychic structures (i.e. the id, ego, and superego) and by unconscious motives or conflicts from early childhood.
Individual	Emphasizes higher human motives and views personality as the individual's complete experience rather than as having separate parts.
Situational	Suggests that personality is not consistent but is merely a response to the situation. We learn to behave in ways that are appropriate to the situation through reinforcement.
Interactive	Combines the situational and trait approaches, so suggests that people have a tendency to behave in certain ways but that this is moderated by the demands of different situations.

tions they are in, and we tend to overestimate the importance of personality in explaining another's behaviour (*fundamental attribution error*—see Chapter 9). However, the situational and behavioural approaches may go too far when they suggest that all variation in behaviour is determined by situational factors or conditioned by patterns of reinforcement. If this were the case then we would not be able to think of examples of when someone else responded differently from how we would have ourselves in an identical situation.

Approaches to personality also vary in the degree to which they see people as *types* or as having more or less of certain *traits*. Type theories tend to emphasize the similarities between people whereas trait approaches stress the differences between individuals and their inherent uniqueness. Eysenck's approach combines both: he used complex statistical techniques to analyse and group together the hundreds of traits shown by large numbers of people (e.g. optimistic, aggressive, lazy). Initially he came up with two groupings in the form of dimensions: introversion–extroversion and stability–neuroticism, and he has since added a third, intelligence–psychoticism, which is unrelated to the other two dimensions. Each dimension is made up of a number of traits and someone who is high on one trait is thought likely to be high on the other traits in that dimension—giving an overall type. Eysenck's theory of personality is illustrated in Figure 7.1.

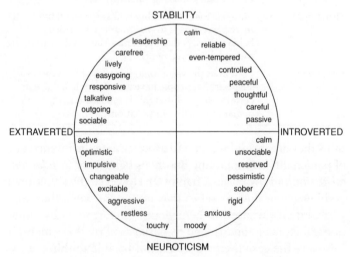

Figure 7.1. Eysenck's personality types

Most people score somewhere in the middle on the introversion–extroversion and neuroticism–stability dimensions, but the majority score lower on psychoticism. Eysenck proposed a biological basis to his theory; suggesting that these personality dimensions were related to biological differences in brain functioning. For example, he proposed that extroverts have lower *cortical arousal* (activity level in the area of the brain that is thought to be responsible for moderating arousal levels) and thus they seek more stimulation and excitement than introverts. In contrast, introverts are thought to be more socially conforming, more sensitive to reinforcement, have lower sensory thresholds, and therefore feel pain more easily. However, there is only limited support for biological differences between different personality types. A psychological test has been developed to measure the dimensions of Eysenck's theory and it uses questions such as 'do you like talking to people so much that you never miss the opportunity to talk to a stranger?' and 'can you easily get some life into a dull party?' to indicate extroversion. Answering 'yes' to questions such as 'do you often worry about things you shouldn't have done or said?' and 'are you troubled by feelings of inferiority?' is taken to indicate greater neuroticism.

What use are psychological tests?

One of the main motivations behind the development of psychological tests measuring attributes such as personality and intelligence has been to be able to predict behaviour. However, the evidence suggests that personality and intelligence may not be as fixed as the concept of psychometric testing suggests. While there is evidence that some personality traits remain relatively stable, particularly after adolescence and early adulthood, there is mixed evidence about whether such personality traits predict the individual's actual behaviour in a given situation. This *consistency paradox* reflects the fact that we tend to see other people as being relatively consistent, as in 'John is the outgoing type', yet research studies found that such traits did not predict a person's actual behaviour in a given situation very well. Examining behaviour across a range of situations shows that personality traits predict behaviour better at the general level (i.e. John was outgoing in the majority of situations), and similarly we can predict an equal number of heads and tails when repeatedly tossing a coin, without being able to predict the outcome of the next toss. In this case, behaviour is influenced by many variables—not only by external ones but also by internal ones such as mood and fatigue.

There has also been much interest in whether IQ predicts behaviour. While there is a relationship between IQ and aspects of intelligent behaviour such as job performance, it is not a strong relationship and within most occupations there is a wide range of IQs. In fact, some studies suggest that socio-economic background is a better predictor of future academic and occupational success than IQ. A long-term study of children with very high IQs found that some became very successful adults but others did not, and there were no differences in IQ between the two groups. There were, however, great differences in motivation: the more successful ones had much more ambition and drive to succeed.

Although psychologists have made significant advances in quantifying and measuring the differences between people, some caution is needed in using such information. In interpreting any single test score it is vital to remember that many factors may have influenced it, including genetic potential, experience, motivation, and conditions of testing. Thus, single scores such as those provided by an IQ test cannot be seen as defining the limit of a person's ability; rather they should be viewed as an indication of their current level, or the approximate range within which they would generally fall. Other dangers associated with psychometric testing arise from value judgements about certain scores—for example, it may be implied that higher scores are better, and thus that people who achieve them are 'superior'. In its most extreme form, this argument can be used for social and political purposes to support ideas such as eugenics and to discourage people with lower IQs from reproducing. But generally speaking, knowing more about how to measure the ways in which people differ according to dimensions such as intelligence and personality has helped us to understand more about the number of contributing variables, the potential for change, and the relationship to achievement.

References

Cattell, R. B. (1963). 'Theory of fluid and crystallized intelligence: a critical experiment'. *Journal of Educational Psychology*, 54: 1–22.

Eysenck, H. J. (1965). *Fact and Fiction in Psychology*. Harmondsworth, Penguin Books Ltd.

8 What happens when things go wrong? Abnormal Psychology

The previous chapters have been concerned with typical human behaviour, and with the individual variation within what is considered normal. In contrast, abnormal psychology is concerned with behaviour that is atypical and with mental disorders and disabilities. Despite this contrast, the information that has arisen from the study of normal behaviour has helped us to understand abnormal behaviour. It is only by understanding how the processes involved in normal functioning work (e.g. cognition, perception, memory, emotion, learning, personality, development, and social relationships) that we can begin to understand what happens when they go wrong. This chapter will look at how we define 'abnormal' behaviour, how we categorize it and attempt to understand it.

What is 'abnormal' behaviour?

Extreme forms of abnormal behaviour are easy to recognize, but the exact line of demarcation between what is normal and what is not is much less clear. For example, it is normal to feel sad after losing someone close to you, but how intensely and for how long? Where does normal grief end and abnormal grief or clinical depression begin? It would be considered abnormal to keep every receipt you have ever been given, to the point where there is room for little else in your home, but is it also abnormal to keep most receipts for a year or two 'just in case'? Most of us consider it normal to have irrational fears, for example of spiders or public speaking, but are they still normal if they are so severe that they prevent you from working or enjoying life? Furthermore, behaviour that is normal in one situation may be considered abnormal in another: being temporarily possessed by 'God' or spirits and speaking in tongues is considered normal in some religions but in other circumstances it may be interpreted as a sign of serious mental illness. Similarly, historical and cultural factors influence ideas about what is normal, as changes in opinion about sexual practices such as homosexuality show.

There are several different ways of defining abnormal behaviour. *Psychological definitions* of abnormal behaviour emphasize the current utility of the behaviour—if the behaviour causes significant distress or prevents you from meeting important goals or developing meaningful relationships, then it is seen as dysfunctional and worthy of treatment. This approach has difficulty in dealing with people who lack insight into their difficulties such as those who are very depressed and see suicide as a welcome relief, or who believe that their auditory hallucinations are the voice of God warning them that their neighbour is really the devil. Similarly, defining behaviour as abnormal solely on the grounds that it causes great distress is not without difficulties—the behaviour may be entirely normal and it may be only the degree of distress that is abnormal.

Medical definitions of abnormal behaviour see it as a symptom of an underlying disease, the cause of which may or may not be known. That is, behaviour is seen as abnormal if it is thought to be caused by a mental illness such as schizophrenia, depression, or anxiety. The emphasis is on accurate diagnosis of the disease to determine the appropriate, usually pharmacological, treatment. However, lack of agreement or evidence about effective treatments can mean that even if the correct diagnosis is made, there may be no clear implications for treatment. The medical model has been criticized for ignoring the effects of the person's environment and for undermining personal responsibility. It also runs into difficulties when people do not have enough symptoms to qualify for having a particular disease, but have one or two symptoms, such as suspiciousness or social withdrawal, quite severely. Technically they do not have the illness, although their behaviour may appear strikingly abnormal.

Abnormality has also been defined in terms of both *statistical and social norms*—behaviour that is statistically uncommon is seen as abnormal. This approach has been applied to learning disabilities (mental handicap) in that people are judged to be learning disabled if their IQ is in the lowest 2.5 per cent of the population. However, one difficulty for the statistical approach is that many behaviours or attributes that are statistically uncommon are not seen as abnormal, e.g. having an IQ in the top 2.5 per cent! Furthermore, some dysfunctional behaviours, such as depression or anxiety, are so common that they are statistically normal, and what is common in one context may not be in another: a degree of depression is a normal response to bereavement but not to winning the lottery. Similarly, behaviour that deviates from what is typical for the social context may be seen as abnormal. Although this approach takes the person's environment into account, it is dependent upon prevailing social and moral attitudes. For example, in Victorian England people could be hospitalized for kissing in a public place, or more recently, some governments have viewed political dissent as abnormal behaviour.

Existential approaches view abnormal behaviour as an inevitable response to an abnormal world, either in terms of the person's immediate world as in their family, or in societal terms. For example, it may be a response to conflicting demands, such as to show respect and affection while on the receiving end of cruelty and humiliation. This also accounts for the fact that people's abnormal behaviour may not be as much of a problem for themselves as it is for those around them. The delusion that one is a very important or famous person may give the person who has the belief a boost, but cause problems for others.

Normalizing or *health-based* approaches try to specify normal behaviour or healthy psychological functioning and then to define abnormal behaviour by contrast. Mental health is thought to involve characteristics such as accurate perception of reality (both of one's own capabilities and of the external world), some degree of self-knowledge and awareness of one's feelings and motives, autonomy and confidence in the ability to exert self-control, a sense of self-worth and self-acceptance, the ability to form close and satisfying relationships that are not destructive to either person, and being fairly competent in one's environment.

None of the approaches to defining abnormal behaviour is completely satisfactory, and it may be better to combine elements of the different definitions. One combined approach that incorporates elements of both social and psychological well-being suggests that while none of the following attributes are necessary or sufficient for behaviour to be seen as abnormal, they tend to indicate abnormality:

irrationality and incomprehensibility; unpredictability and loss of control; personal and social maladaptiveness; suffering; unconventionality; violation of moral and ideal standards; and causing distress to others observing the behaviour.

This approach has the advantage of being more flexible, but a potential disadvantage is that it allows a greater degree of subjectivity. Psychologists have recognized that part of the difficulty in defining abnormal behaviour arises from the fact that such behaviour may have reflected an entirely adaptive response in an earlier environment. For example, a child who learns to avoid punishment or criticism by keeping quiet may be showing behaviour that is functional in those circumstances. However, if the reticence persists into adulthood, then such behaviour may become dysfunctional in that it prevents the person from forming relationships with others.

Classifying abnormality

There are advantages and disadvantages inherent in attempting to classify the many different forms of abnormal behaviour into types. One potential advantage is that, if different types of abnormal behaviour have different causes, then we may understand more about them by grouping together people with a certain type of abnormal behaviour, and looking for other similarities in their behaviour or history. For example, by studying many people who had panic attacks, similarities in their styles of thinking were noticed— people who experienced panic attacks tended to interpret their bodily sensations as signs of impending catastrophe. Those who had panic attacks were much more likely to interpret feelings of tightness in the chest (a common symptom of anxiety) as a sign of heart disease or impending suffocation. The evidence now suggests that these catastrophic interpretations of body sensations play a causal role in bringing on panic attacks.

Classifying and labelling different types of abnormal behaviour into *diagnoses*, which are medical names for disorders (e.g. terms such as *bulimia nervosa* or *social phobia*), acts as a kind of medical shorthand in that it conveys a lot of information in relatively few words. For example, we know that people with social phobia are overly concerned about doing or saying something that they think will embarrass or humiliate them in front of others, and consequently try to avoid certain social situations or interactions. We can also bring to bear information from treating other socially phobic patients, for example about what type of treatment is likely to be effective. But when using diagnostic labels it is important to avoid stereotyping. The danger is that once people are given the label of a 'phobic', they may be seen as identical to other phobic patients and important details about their phobia and personal responses to it may be ignored. It can also be dehumanizing in that often it is the person rather than the illness that is labelled, as in 'he's a schizophrenic' rather than 'he is suffering from schizophrenia', as if all people with schizophrenia had identical personalities.

Many mental health professionals use a standard method of classifying patients' behaviour both for research purposes and in clinical practice, so that it is clear that people working in different places or settings know that they are referring to the same thing. Currently, the most commonly used classification system is the fourth edition of the *Diagnostic and Statistical Manual of Mental Disorders* (DSM-IV for short), which is produced by the American Psychiatric Association. Some examples of the types of abnormal behaviour covered in DSM-IV are shown in Table 8.1.

In order to meet the criteria for diagnoses according to DSM-IV, the person must have been experiencing the symptoms for a specified amount of time, and the particular symptoms listed must cause them significant distress or impairment in functioning. So there are not 'all or none' definitions and it is hardly surprising that untrained people suspect that they have every diagnosis in the book when they first read the list.

Explaining abnormal behaviour

Throughout history abnormal behaviour has been attributed to a wide variety of causes, from dietary deficiencies to the

TABLE 8.1. Different types of abnormal behaviour

Category	Examples of specific disorders
Schizophrenic and other psychotic disorders	A group of disorders characterized by psychotic symptoms—loss of contact with reality as in hallucinations or delusions, marked disturbances of thought and perception, and bizarre behaviour.
Anxiety disorders	Several disorders in which the main symptoms are of anxiety either in response to a particular stimulus as in phobias, or more diffuse anxiety as in generalized anxiety. Many of these disorders involve panic attacks, defined in terms of the sudden and intense onset of a number of anxiety symptoms.
Mood disorders	Disturbances of normal mood ranging from extreme depression to abnormal elation (*mania*), or alternating between the two (*manic depression*).
Somatoform disorders	Physical symptoms, such as pain or paralysis, for which no physical basis can be found, and in which psychological factors appear to play a role, e.g. a mother who loses the use of her right arm when her son joins the army, but regains it when he is home on leave. Also included in this category is hypochondriasis, which is excessive concern with health and a preoccupation with disease, often involving the erroneous belief that one has a fatal disease.
Dissociative disorders	Disorders involving a disruption in the usually integrated functions of consciousness, memory, identity, or perception, for emotional reasons. Included in this category are multiple personality disorder and amnesia, e.g. forgetting being involved in a traumatic experience.
Sexual and gender identity disorders	Includes problems of sexual preferences such as sexual interest in children (*paedophilia*), or in objects (*fetishism*), problems in gender identity such as *transsexualism* (the belief that you are trapped in a body of the wrong sex), and sexual dysfunctions (e.g. impotence).

Eating disorders	Disorders characterized by severe disturbances in eating behaviour, e.g. anorexia and bulimia nervosa.
Sleep disorders	Disorders involving abnormalities in the amount, quality, or timing of sleep (e.g. insomnia), or abnormal behaviour or physiological events occurring during sleep (e.g. nightmares, night terrors, sleepwalking).
Impulse control disorders	Disorders involving the failure to resist an impulse, drive, or temptation, e.g. *kleptomania* involving impulsive stealing for no personal gain, or *trichotillomania* involving habitual pulling out of one's hair for pleasure or tension relief.
Personality disorders	Enduring patterns of inner experience and behaviour that are pervasive and inflexible, lead to distress or impairment, and deviate from social norms, e.g. *narcissistic personality disorder* involves a pattern of grandiosity, need for admiration, and lack of empathy; *obsessive-compulsive personality* is characterized by preoccupation with orderliness, perfectionism, and control.
Substance-related disorders	Excessive use of, or dependence on, alcohol or drugs.
Factitious disorders	Physical or psychological symptoms that are intentionally produced or feigned in order to assume a 'sick role' or gain other benefits such as financial benefits or reduced responsibility.

phases of the moon or evil spirits. More recently investigators have used scientific methods such as careful observation and hypothesis testing to propose several different theories to account for abnormal behaviour. Not surprisingly, these explanations are quite closely related to the different views of personality that are outlined in Table 7.1. Explanations of abnormal behaviour vary in the degree to which they focus on the past or present, whether they are based on psychological theory or medical models, whether the views of the therapist and patient are given equal weight, and in the treatments they advocate.

It is common in psychiatry to use a *medical model* which sees abnormal behaviour as the result of physical or mental illnesses that are caused by biochemical or physical dysfunctions in the brain or body, some of which may be inherited. One of the early successes of the medical model in explaining abnormal behaviour was the discovery that *general paresis*, a debilitating form of dementia that was common earlier this century, was a long-term consequence of infection with syphilis. The main tasks of treatment in the medical model are making the correct diagnosis and administering appropriate treatment—for example, physical treatments such as medication (e.g. anti-depressant or anti-psychotic drugs), or psychosurgery (surgical techniques to destroy or disconnect specific areas of the brain) or ECT (electroconvulsive therapy). Recent advances in pharmacotherapy mean that modern drug treatments do not have the debilitating side-effects that were associated with their predecessors. While these drug treatments are effective for many people, we are still some distance from having medications that work for everyone, and are free from side-effects. Both psychosurgery and ECT were widely used before the advent of drug therapies, and their relatively indiscriminate use gained them a bad reputation. In modern psychiatry ECT and psychosurgery are used in a much more discriminate and refined manner. Psychosurgery is used with greater precision and only as a last resort, when other treatments have failed, in the treatment of chronic severe pain, depression, or obsessive-compulsive disorder. Similarly, ECT is used to induce seizures which affect the balance of chemicals in the brain. Although the practice of ECT has been described as barbaric and inhumane, the use of muscle relaxants and anaesthesia mean that it can be given with a minimum of discomfort, and research demonstrates that it can be effective in alleviating depression in patients who have not responded to any other treatment and who may be at risk of suicide.

Psychodynamic approaches to understanding abnormality are based on the work of Sigmund Freud and have been expanded by many others. In brief, psychodynamic approaches see abnormal behaviour as arising from conflicts between instinctual drives, which lead to anxieties, which are in turn dealt with by *defence mechanisms*, or strategies used to avoid or reduce the experience of the anxiety, and to protect the person's ego. Treatment often focuses on the patient's early life experiences and involves the therapist helping to reveal the patient's unconscious motives and to resolve the original conflicts. Psychodynamic therapists developed techniques such as *free association* where patients are encouraged to say whatever comes into their minds, and the therapist interprets the associations. They base their interpretations of patients' distress, and signs of it such as their dreams and their feelings towards the therapist (*transference*), on psychodynamic theories and models of behaviour.

In contrast to the psychodynamic approach, humanistic psychotherapy focuses on the present and views the patients as being in the best position to understand their problems. Humanistic approaches see the person's sense of self as critical in promoting personal growth and well-being. The aim of therapy is to promote self-esteem and self-acceptance, which may have been lowered by unhappy events or difficult relationships. Therapy is an enabling process in which the therapist enables patients to reveal their problems in an atmosphere of 'unconditional positive regard'—that is, the therapist is genuinely non-judgemental towards patients and shows warmth and empathy for them.

A second set of approaches to understanding abnormality that focus on the present are behavioural and, more recently, cognitive-behavioural approaches. Initially the behavioural approach asserted that it was not necessary to understand the origins of abnormal behaviour in order to treat it—psychological symptoms were seen as maladaptive behaviour patterns which were learnt, and thus, could be unlearnt. Such radical behavioural approaches focused solely on observable behaviour. Internal events and meanings and the patient's history were largely ignored. Techniques of therapy included reconditioning by, for example, *systematic desensitization*, in which the patient is taught relaxation techniques and uses them to reduce their anxiety during exposure to a hierarchy of increasingly threatening situations. In this way situations that were once associated with anxiety subsequently become associated with relaxation and are no longer feared. Nowadays, behavioural approaches are often combined with cognitive approaches.

Cognitive-behavioural approaches look both at the patient's observable behaviour and also at their internal interpretations of the situation (cognitions). They take into account both history and current patterns of behaviour, and they also draw upon the findings of experimental research in cognitive psychology. Adding cognitive elements has been shown to increase both the efficacy of and compliance with behavioural treatments. For example, an agoraphobic patient, whom we shall call Sarah, was too terrified even to contemplate any treatment involving *exposure* (facing the feared stimulus—in this case, going outside). The therapist used cognitive techniques to discover that Sarah believed that if she went outside, she would be so overwhelmed by anxiety that she would have palpitations which could induce a heart attack. The therapist helped Sarah to think about her symptoms anew, by providing medical evidence indicating that it was highly unlikely that Sarah's symptoms were due to impending heart failure, and by examining what happened to Sarah during an attack, which indicated that the palpitations were a symptom of anxiety rather than of heart disease. Sarah was sufficiently reassured by this information to begin an exposure programme. Later in therapy, a *behavioural experiment* was used to test Sarah's prediction that anxiety-induced palpitations could bring on heart failure—Sarah tested whether or not these palpitations would lead to heart failure by doing everything she could to bring on a heart attack during the palpitations (e.g. staying in a hot room, doing vigorous exercise). When this did not bring on a heart attack, Sarah was finally convinced that her palpitations were due to anxiety, and would not cause any permanent damage.

Clearly, attempting to differentiate abnormal from normal behaviour is not straightforward: what is considered abnormal is somewhat subjective and depends on the context, current values, and norms, and on the way in which both normal and abnormal behaviour are conceptualized. Also, different ways of understanding normal personality and normal behaviour will influence how abnormal behaviour is understood and treated. Many factors contribute to causing abnormal behaviour including genetics, early experiences, learning history, biochemical changes in the brain, unconscious conflicts, recent stressful or traumatic events, and thinking styles. Systems for classifying abnormal behaviour into different types have been devised to aid communication and understanding, but their validity has often been questioned.

Despite these difficulties, abnormal psychology has provided some understanding of abnormal behaviour, and of how to help others in difficulty. While such treatments are helpful in ameliorating distress, they do not give us the secret to happiness, but focus on helping the person to return to a 'normal' state. In considering which treatment is best, it must be remembered that it is difficult accurately to compare the efficacy of different approaches, particularly as some approaches are not very amenable to testing. How does one measure the degree of unconscious conflict or self-actualization? The most demonstrably effective treatments are those that are based on testable theories and that have been evaluated using all the props of science: independent assessment, experiments designed to test specific hypotheses, multiple standardized measures, repeated measurement, and appropriate comparison groups. At present, there is evidence that both pharmacological and psychological treatments can be effective in ameliorating distressing symptoms, and psychological treatments such as cognitive-behaviour therapy may have an advantage over pharmacological treatments in terms of *relapse rates* (the proportion of people who deteriorate or relapse once treatment has finished).

Abnormal psychology has been able to develop in the way that it has partly because of advances made in other areas of psychology. Examples include understanding the ways in which perception and attention are influenced by moods (how being fearful keeps one on the lookout for dangers or *hypervigilant*); how one might be able to detect a signal without being aware of doing so, and become distressed without understanding why; how memories can be inaccurate as well as accurate; and how hard it can be to withstand the pressure of a peer group. Future developments in abnormal psychology, whether they are directed towards improving treatments or preventing problems arising, will therefore not take place in isolation, and the ways in which they are applied will need to be subjected to similarly rigorous scientific and ethical standards. Abnormal psychologists attempt to ensure that the facts on which their theories and practices are based are sufficiently well founded, and applied in demonstrably unbiased ways, without coercion, that do not intentionally foster dependency or create additional problems. For this reason ethical standards for the application of treatments in abnormal psychology have been developed and are constantly being revised in the light of new developments— both scientific and cultural.

Reference

American Psychiatric Association (1994). *Diagnostic and Statistical Manual of Mental Disorders* (4th edition). Washington, DC, APA.

9 How do we influence each other? Social Psychology

*T*he previous chapters have concentrated on the individual. However, human behaviour can only be properly understood if it is thought of as social in nature: as being directly or indirectly influenced by the behaviour of others. Simply being in the presence of others will normally affect our behaviour: you may do things when you are alone at home that you would not dream of doing in public. Psychologists call this process of behaviour change as a result of being in the presence of others *social facilitation*. One obvious form of social facilitation is competition. In general, people's performance is enhanced if they believe that they are competing with someone else—even if there is no prize. It seems that the mere presence of others, rather than the atmosphere of competition, is the crucial element. Even when people are asked not to compete, they work faster when they can see others working (the *co-action effect*), or when they are being observed by others (the *audience effect*).

Experiments have shown that social facilitation can be produced by simply telling subjects that others are performing the same task elsewhere. Hence, your motivation to study for an exam may be increased by telephoning a classmate and finding out that they are already hard at it. Whether or not social facilitation enhances performance depends upon the nature of the task. If the task is simple and well learned performance may improve, but it may deteriorate if the task is complex, novel, or difficult. Social facilitation has been demonstrated in animals too—even cockroaches run faster when they are being watched by their peers!

A more direct form of social influence involves not merely being in the presence of other people but interacting with them and making some attempt to change their behaviour. This could happen when someone tries to influence the group as a whole (*leadership*), when several group members encourage others to adopt a particular attitude (*conformity*), when an authority figure tries to make someone comply with their demands (*obedience*), or when the attitudes of one group influence behaviour towards another group (*prejudice*). This chapter will focus on these four issues as examples of social psychology.

A born leader?

It was originally thought that leadership was a trait that some people possessed and others did not. Hence, comments such as 'he's a born leader'. A number of attributes, such as height, weight, intelligence, confidence, and an attractive appearance, have been proposed as being related to leadership, at least in men. With regard to intelligence, several studies have shown that the typical leader is only slightly more intelligent than the average group member, but in general, psychologists have been unable to find many attributes that consistently distinguish leaders from non-leaders. This may explain why we can all think of leaders who, for example, are not particularly attractive.

Because specific leadership traits are not demonstrable, psychologists have explored other possibilities. First, leadership style has been shown to influence the behaviour and productivity of group members. In general, a democratic style promotes good productivity with the best relationships between group members. An autocratic style, which is more authoritarian and directive, and allows group members less say in decisions, produces as much productivity (provided the leader is present), but tends to lead to poorer relationships and less cooperation between group members. Laissez-faire leadership, which leaves the group to its own devices, results in much less productivity than either a democratic or authoritarian approach. The results of these studies have influenced the development of management strategies in many organizations, encouraging a move away from authoritarian models of management towards the more democratic process of allowing workers to have a say in the running of the organization.

Psychologists have also investigated the situational aspects of leadership, suggesting that leadership is primarily determined by the functions that the group needs a leader to fulfil. Thus, the match between the leader's personal qualities or leadership style and the requirements of the situation is crucial. There is some evidence to support this notion. For example, relationship-oriented leadership is more productive when conditions for the group are neither extremely good nor extremely bad. In contrast, task-oriented leadership, which is directive and controlling, produces greater benefits when the group's conditions are more extreme (either extremely favourable or extremely unfavourable). This may help to account for the increased popularity of dictators as leaders in countries that are experiencing times of extreme hardship. For example, Hitler became popular as Germany was struggling under the weight of reparations after losing the First World War.

In order to find out more about situational influences on leadership, some researchers have studied the effects of putting a random person in a central position. Experiments

have shown that if members of a group are forced to communicate only through one central person, then that person be-
gins to function as a leader. Compared with people occupying
more peripheral positions, people in central positions send
more messages, solve problems faster, make fewer errors, and
are more satisfied with their own and the group's efforts.
People put in positions of leadership tend to accept the
challenge, behave like leaders, and be recognized by others
as leaders. This may explain why people who do not appear to
be natural leaders can nevertheless rise to the occasion: 'some
men are born great, some achieve greatness, and some have
greatness thrust upon them' (*Twelfth Night*, Act 2). Thus, the
qualities that make a good leader vary according to the situation and the nature of the problem faced by the members of
the group in question.

Conformity

Understanding leadership helps to explain the effect of an individual on a group, but the effects of a group on an individual are also more complex than might be supposed. You may
have been in a group situation where your opinion differs
from the majority. In such circumstances you might change
your opinion to conform with the group—particularly if you
are not sure of your own opinion, or if you have reason to believe that the majority has a more valid source of information.
However, what if you are sure that you are correct and the
group is incorrect? Would you yield to social pressure and
conform? Changing one's behaviour or attitudes as a result of
perceived pressure from a person or group of people is called
conformity. You may have noticed that if several people have
already given the same answer to a question, the last person is
unlikely to disagree. Hence, a 'hung jury' is a fairly rare oc-
currence. Conformity has been studied in experiments in
which a person is asked to answer a simple question, after

they have already heard several others give the same wrong answer. It is important that the real subject believes that the other people are answering honestly. Results show that people conform, that is, give the same wrong answer, about 30 per cent of the time.

Why do people do this? It seems that there are several reasons why people change their opinions or behaviour as a result of group pressure. Some people who conformed in these experiments admitted to knowing that they had given an incorrect answer, but gave it because they did not want to appear to be the odd one out, or feared that people would laugh at them, or that they would disrupt the experiment if they did not conform. Others appeared to have internalized the group's opinion and thus, did not realize that they had been influenced by others. This type of conformity, in which the influence of others remains unrecognized, is more common when the task is difficult, or when the other people are perceived as more competent. For example, your opinion about the date of the next election is likely to be influenced more by hearing a group of politicians say that it will be in April, than by hearing a group of shopkeepers say so.

Obedience

Conformity occurs when someone yields to group pressure. Similar effects can be produced by an authority figure, and complying with the demands of an authority figure is called *obedience*. Scientific investigations into obedience were prompted by atrocities of war such as the Holocaust or the killing of Vietnamese civilians at My Lai. In the aftermath of these wars it became apparent that many soldiers, who appeared to be ordinary decent people, had committed atrocious acts. When asked why they had done these things, a common defence was 'I was following orders'. Thus, psychologists became interested in just how far the average person would go, simply because they were told to. Box 9.1 describes one experiment investigating obedience in the general public.

Box 9.1. *Extremes of obedience*

Members of the public, recruited through a newspaper, participated in 'a study of memory'. Subjects were told that they would play the role of 'teacher' and would be teaching a series of word pairs to a 'learner'. Teachers were instructed to press a lever to deliver an electric shock to the learner, for every error made. Teachers saw the learner being strapped into an electrically wired chair with an electrode placed on the wrist, and were convinced of the generator's authenticity by being given a sample shock of 45 volts. Then, seated in front of the generator with 30 switches ranging from '15 volts—mild shock' to '450 volts—Danger: Severe shock', teachers were told to move up a level for each error made. The experimenter remained in the room throughout. In reality, the learner was an actor who did not receive shocks but who had been trained to respond as if he did, and briefed to make many errors. As the shocks became stronger, the actor began to shout and curse. At the level marked 'extreme intensity shock' the actor went quiet and no longer answered questions. Not surprisingly, many of the subjects objected and asked to stop the experiment. The experimenter instructed them to continue. A staggering 65 per cent of the subjects continued right to the end of the shock series (450 volts) and none stopped before 300 volts (when the actor began to kick the adjoining wall). The results of this experiment suggest that ordinary people will go very far indeed when they are told to by someone in a position of authority.

Milgram, 1974

What produces such obedience? One suggestion is that obedience to authority is vital for communal life and may have been built into our genetic make-up during evolution. Indeed many aspects of civilized life, such as the legal, military, and school systems, rely on people obeying the directions of authority figures. However, psychological factors may also influence obedience. Social norms, such as being polite, may have contributed to making it difficult for the subjects to refuse to continue, particularly once they had started. Refusing to continue would have meant admitting that what they had already been doing was wrong, and could imply that they thought badly of the experimenter. This may make it easier to understand why so few people disobey orders during war, when punishments for disobedience are more serious than merely offending someone. The presence of the experimenter also increased obedience: when instructions were issued by telephone obedience dropped from 65 per cent to 21 per cent. Furthermore, several people cheated by giving weaker shocks. So obedience is at least partly dependent upon continued surveillance.

Two other factors, which are also relevant to the obedience seen during wars, affected obedience in these experiments. First, people are more prepared to inflict pain on another person if they can distance themselves from the victim. If the teacher had to respond to errors by forcing the learner's hand down onto a shock plate, obedience was much lower than when the teacher did not have to see or touch the learner. This has parallels with modern warfare in which it is now possible to kill at the touch of a button without ever having to see the victims' suffering. Indeed, it is psychologically easier to kill millions with a nuclear bomb than to kill one person face to face. Second, believing the violence to be a means to an end in a worthy cause, or *ideological justification*, affects obedience. In the experiments, people thought that they were acting in the interests of scientific research. When the experiment was repeated without the associations of a prestigious university, fewer people were prepared to obey the instructions. Similarly, in war, many soldiers supposedly believe that following orders will be for the greater good of their countrymen, and their training involves cultivating attitudes that facilitate aggressive acts, often by dehumanizing the enemy.

When asked in advance, most people are adamant that they would not conform or obey instructions to deliver such electric shocks. The fact that most people do indeed conform or obey suggests that we are not good at predicting our own behaviour. This discrepancy between what we think we would do and what we actually do is a good example of our tendency to overestimate the importance of personality factors and underestimate the importance of situational influences (the *fundamental attribution error*). While obedience and conformity may not be seen as very desirable, they clearly contribute to the cohesiveness that enables us to live in a civilized society. For example, there could be no law enforcement without obedience and no democracy without some conformity.

Prejudice

In addition to looking at the influences of groups on individuals, social psychology is also concerned with the influences of one group on another group. The blue eyes-brown eyes experiment (Box 9.2) shows how belonging to a particular group can change one's behaviour.

Box 9.2. *Are blue or brown eyes better?*

Pupils were told by their teacher that those with brown eyes were more intelligent and 'better' people. The teacher then gave the brown-eyed children special privileges such as sitting at the front of the class. Behaviour in both groups changed: the blue-eyed children showed signs of lowered self-esteem and depressed mood, and did less well in their work, while the brown-eyed children became critical and oppressive towards their 'inferiors'. After a few days, when the teacher said that she had made a mistake, and the blue-eyed children were the superior ones, the behaviour patterns quickly reversed, with the brown-eyed children becoming more depressed. Of course, the rationale for the study was explained to the children once it was over.

Aronson and Osherow, 1980

Despite its artificiality, this experiment has many implications for prejudice in the real world. Prejudices are relatively enduring (usually negative) attitudes about a group that are extended towards members of that group. Prejudice often involves *stereotyping*. Stereotyping is the tendency to categorize people according to some readily identifiable characteristic such as age, race, sex, or occupation, and then to attribute to the individual the characteristics that are supposedly typical of members of that group. For example, someone who is prejudiced against women may believe that women are stupid and weak, and they will apply this belief to every woman they encounter. While the stereotypes involved in prejudices may contain a grain of truth (for example, on average women are physically weaker than men), they are frequently overly general—some women are stronger than some men—overly rigid—not all women are weak or stupid—or simply inaccurate—there is no evidence that women are less intelligent than men.

Many forms of prejudice have been demonstrated in different groups across the world and social psychologists have investigated the psychological factors underlying them. Again, it seems that both personality factors and situational influences contribute to the development of prejudices. The blue eyes-brown eyes experiment suggested that prejudice can be created simply by giving one group privileges over another. Similarly, when two groups are set up in competition for the same resources prejudice easily develops, as in the Robbers' Cave Experiment (Box 9.3).

Several sources of evidence show that competition for resources can lead to prejudice. For example, the number of racially motivated lynchings in the southern states of the USA is said to have increased with financial hardship, and decreased in more prosperous years. Prejudice might also arise out of a general need to see oneself positively: people come to see any groups to which they belong more positively than

---

Box 9.3. *Robbers' Cave Experiment*

Twenty-two 11-year-old boys participated in this study of cooperative behaviour at a summer camp (Robbers' Cave).

Stage one: The boys were divided into two groups without knowing of each others' existence. Each group chose a name, the Rattlers and the Eagles, and formed a group identity by wearing caps and t-shirts showing their names. Each group engaged in cooperative activities and developed standards of group behaviour such as swimming in the nude or not mentioning homesickness.

Stage 2: An element of competition was introduced. The groups became aware of each other and competed for prizes in a grand tournament. Conflict quickly developed with each group attacking the other after losing a round of the competition.

Stage 3: Conflict resolution through cooperative activities. These activities involved goals that both groups wanted but could only be achieved through cooperation, for example, pooling funds to rent a minibus. This succeeded in eliminating prejudices against members of the other group, and towards members of their own group.

Sherif, Harvey, White, Hood, and Sherif, 1961

---

other groups. In this manner they develop positive prejudices about their own groups and negative prejudices about other groups (*ethnocentrism*). It has also been suggested that prejudice is a form of *scapegoating* in which aggression is directed towards a scapegoat (usually a socially approved or legitimized target), because it is not possible to direct one's aggression toward the real target—for fear of the consequences or because they are not accessible.

Situational factors clearly influence the development of prejudices. However, several studies have found that people who hold prejudices tend to have certain personality characteristics such as being less flexible and more authoritarian. This relationship between personality characteristics and the tendency to develop prejudices may help to explain why two people who have had similar experiences can have differing levels of prejudice.

Psychologists have used their knowledge about the psychological factors involved in prejudice to look at methods for reducing prejudice. Initially, it was thought that increased contact and decreased segregation would help. The absence of direct contact with another group leads to *autistic hostility*—ignorance of another group produces a failure to understand the reasons for their actions, and provides no opportunities to find out if negative interpretations of their behaviour are incorrect. Thus, contact between opposing groups is needed before prejudices can be reduced. However, contact based on inequity, as when male bosses employ female secretaries or cleaners, may serve to reinforce stereotypes. Furthermore, because inequity and competition for scarce resources facilitate the development of prejudice, contact to reduce prejudice should be based on equality and encourage the pursuit of common goals rather than competition.

We have looked at social facilitation, leadership, conformity, obedience, and prejudice and been able to see that our thoughts, feelings, and behaviours are influenced by others. What can be concluded from these studies and what use are these conclusions? Studies of social facilitation and leadership suggest that certain working conditions can enhance workers' productivity and satisfaction, and this information has been useful to employers. Studies of obedience and conformity show that we are much more likely to be influenced by pressure from others than we realize, and they provide a framework for understanding why we are susceptible to such pressures. Greater understanding of the factors contributing to obedience and conformity has been useful both in situations where conformity and obedience are desirable, such as in the military forces, and in situations where it is important that people stay true to their own opinions. For example, some American states now use juries of six rather than twelve as social psychologists' findings suggest that smaller groups are less likely to produce undue pressure to conform. The psychological study of prejudice has identified some of the underlying factors and facilitated the development of more effective programmes to reduce prejudice and conflict between different groups.

This chapter has introduced some of the issues that social psychologists are interested in, and some of the methods they use to investigate them. Many interesting areas of social psychology have not been covered here, such as group dynamics, bystander intervention, behaviour of crowds, impression formation, and interpersonal attraction. Both antisocial behaviour, such as football hooliganism, and pro-social behaviour, such as acts of altruism, are of interest. The major challenge for the future of social psychology is to find out more about the many factors that help to predict, control, or modify (increase or decrease) both types of behaviour.

References

Aronson, E., and Osherow, N. (1980). 'Co-operation, pro-social behaviour and academic performance: experiments in the desegregated classroom'. *Applied Social Psychology Annual*, 1: 163–96.

Milgram, S. (1974). *Obedience to Authority: An Experimental View*. New York, Harper & Row.

Sherif, M., Harvey, O. J., White, B. J., Hood, W. R., and Sherif, C. W. (1961). *Intergroup Conflict and Co-operation: The Robbers Cave Experiment*. University of Oklahoma Press.

10 What is psychology for?

As well as being an academic discipline psychology has many practical uses. Academic psychologists are likely to specialize in one area of psychology, and to carry out research to further 'the science of mental life'. Their findings help us to understand, explain, predict, or modify what goes on in the mind as the control centre for cognition, affect, and behaviour (what we think, feel, and do). They may also develop theories and hypotheses to test, and carry out original research in their applied settings, so that developments in the academic and professional fields can influence each other, with especially productive results when communication between them is good. For example, experimental laboratory-based work demonstrating that animals would complete quite complex tasks, or series of tasks, in order to gain a reward, together with research into the application of these methods in humans, stimulated the development of *token economy* programmes. These work by rewarding behaviour that you want to increase with tokens which can later be exchanged for 'goodies' or privileges. Such programmes have been used successfully in the rehabilitation of offenders, and in helping people become more independent after spending years in hospital. Alternatively, the observations of professional psychologists may stimulate academic interest. For example, psychologists working in hospitals noticed that some patients with auditory hallucinations seemed to have fewer hallucinations if they wore an ear-plug. This observation prompted valuable research into the relationship between hearing and auditory hallucinations.

Where do professional psychologists work?

Psychologists are likely to be interested in most aspects of human functioning, and in some of the ways in which animals function too. Hence there are many fields in which they work as applied or professional psychologists. Clinical or health psychologists work in health care settings such as hospitals, clinics, doctors' offices, or in other community settings. Clinical psychologists mainly use psychological techniques to help people overcome difficulties and distress. Their postgraduate training enables them to provide therapy or advice, to evaluate psychological and other interventions, and to use their research skills to develop new ones, to teach and supervise others, and to contribute to the planning, development, and management of services generally. Health psychologists are more concerned with the psychological aspects of their patients' physical health, and apply their knowledge to aid the treatment or prevention of illness and disability. For example, devising education programmes about AIDS or diet; finding out about how best to communicate with patients, or helping people to manage health-related problems such as post-operative recovery or living with a chronic illness such as diabetes.

Professional psychologists also work outside health care settings. For example, forensic psychologists work with prison, probation, or police services, and use their skills in helping to solve crimes, predict the behaviour of offenders or suspects, and in rehabilitating offenders. Educational psychologists specialize in all aspects of schooling, such as looking at the determinants of learning and adjustment, or at solving educational problems. Environmental psychologists are interested in the interactions between people and their environment, and work in areas such as town planning, ergonomics, and designing housing so as to reduce crime. Sports psychologists try to help athletes maximize their performance, and develop training schemes and ways of dealing with the stresses of competition.

Many areas of business and commerce also use professional psychologists. Occupational psychologists consider all aspects of working life, including selection, training, staff morale, ergonomics, managerial issues, job satisfaction, motivation, and sick leave. Frequently they are employed by companies to enhance the satisfaction and/or performance of employees. Consumer psychologists focus on marketing issues such as advertising, shopping behaviour, market research, and the development of new products for changing markets.

People who have learned about psychology at school or at university but who have not completed a professional training in the subject often find their knowledge of psychology useful in both their personal lives and their work. It is hardly surprising that there are many advantages in knowing something about how the mind works and in knowing how to determine whether intuitions or preconceptions about its workings, which are predominantly based on introspection, are justified. Both the findings of psychologists and the methods they use to discover things are potentially useful in a range of professional roles such as teaching, social work, policing, nursing and medicine, research for TV or radio programmes, political advising or analysis, journalism or writing, management and personnel, developing methods of communication and information technology, and also training or caring for animals, their health, or the environments they require for survival. The discipline of psychology teaches skills that are widely applicable as well as providing a training in thinking scientifically about mental life—about thoughts, feelings, and behaviour.

Uses and abuses of psychology

People frequently make assumptions about what psychologists are able to do—for example, that they can tell what you are thinking from your body language, or read your mind. While such assumptions are understandable, they are not correct. Psychologists can, as we have seen, study aspects of thinking, use rewards to change behaviour, give advice to people who are distressed, and predict future behaviour with some accuracy. Nevertheless they cannot read people's minds, or manipulate people against their will, and they have not yet drawn up a blueprint for happiness.

Psychology can also be misused, as indeed can any other scientific body of information. Some of its misuses are relatively trivial, as in providing superficial answers to difficult questions, such as how to become a good parent, but some are not at all trivial: for example, treating people with certain political opinions as mentally ill. Psychologists have also been accused of such things as fostering 'psycho babble', or pseudo-scientific, jargon-ridden pronouncements and advice, and of developing poorly constructed schemes supposedly based on sound psychological principles. One critic of psychology, commenting on the recent increase in team building by means of adventure courses, said, 'Psychologists, past masters at convening conferences in order to state the obvious, have at last turned their attention to this most bizarre manifestation of late twentieth century corporate sadism.' The researchers had 'discovered' that those 'who do not shine on the raft-building front are likely to return to their offices with their confidence in shreds'. Of course, the reason why such courses are on the increase may have more to do with financial benefits than with psychological decisions.

The fact that psychology, like any other discipline, can be misunderstood and misused does not detract from its value. However, psychology *is* in a special position because it is a subject about which everyone has some inside information, and about which everyone can express an opinion based on personal information and subjective experience. An example may help to illustrate the point. Having spent many years researching various kinds of unhappiness, psychologists are now turning their attention to more positive emotions, and have conducted surveys into the happiness of women in their marriages. A representative survey of American women reported that half of those married five years or more said they were 'very happy' or 'completely satisfied' with their marriages and 10 per cent reported having had an affair during their current marriage. In contrast to this, Shere Hite, in her report on *Women and Love*, claimed that 70 per cent of women married five years or more were having affairs and 95 per cent of women felt emotionally harassed by the men they loved. Unlike the results of the first survey, these findings were widely reported in the media, and Shere Hite herself placed great weight on the results because 4,500 women had responded to her survey. However there are two major problems with her work. First, less than 5 per cent of the people sampled responded (so we do not know the views of over 95 per cent of them), and second, only women belonging to women's organizations were contacted in the first place. Thus the respondents (the small percentage of women belonging to women's organizations who chose to respond to the survey) were not representative of the relevant population of women. This kind of reporting raises problems as we know that people have a tendency to accept information that fits with their hunches or preconceptions, and that attention is easily grabbed by startling, novel, or alarming information.

The point is that psychology is not being led by hunches, and nor is it common sense. In order properly to understand psychological findings people need to know something about how to evaluate the status and nature of the information they are given. Psychologists can, and do, contribute to debates such as that about marriages and their happiness, and they can help us to ask the kinds of questions that can be answered using scientific methods. Not 'are marriages happy?' but 'what do women who have been married five years or more report about the happiness of their marriages?' The scientific, methodological nature of psychology therefore determines what psychology is for—hence the importance of developing appropriate methods of inquiry, reporting results in demonstrably objective ways, and also educating others about the discipline of psychology.

Like any science, the nature of psychology has been, and is being, determined by the scientific methods and technology at its disposal. In the same way, the design of the bridges and buildings being built, and the speed with which information spreads between people far apart, are determined by technological developments. For instance, statistical and sophisticated computerized programmes help psychologists ensure that their surveys accurately reflect the facts. Surveys of large groups of people could tell us much about specific aspects of happiness, provided they were representative, carried out properly, interpreted with caution, and reported in an unbiased way. For a survey to be representative all relevant groups of people—urban or rural, black or white, rich or poor, and so on, should have an equal chance of being selected, and the sample should pick up people in the same proportions as in the population from which the sample is drawn. Developments in computer technology help psychologists to carry out such random sampling procedures, and to check that their random sample is truly representative of the population. A sample of equal numbers of black and white people would be as unrepresentative in Zambia as it would in France. Statistical considerations are paramount, and these suggest, for example, that a random sample of 1,500 people could provide a reasonably accurate estimate of the views of 100 million people—provided it were representative. Having 4,500 people in the survey does not make it more accurate than a sample of 1,500 people if the composition of the sample differs in important ways from that of the population about whom conclusions are drawn. Once again psychology is in an especially difficult position because some aspects of its technology are generally available. Anyone can conduct a survey. Not anyone can build a bridge. Knowing how to do it properly is equally important.

What next? Progress and complexity

A hundred years ago psychology as we know it today hardly existed. Great advances have been made in all aspects of the subject—and more can be expected. For example, we now know that, to a large extent, we construct our experience of the world and what happens in it, and do not just use our faculties of perception, attention, learning, and memory to provide us with a passive reflection of external reality. Our mental life turns out to be far more active than was supposed by the early psychologists who began by documenting its structures and functions, and it has been shaped over the millennia by evolutionary forces of adaptation to be this way. Psychologists have enabled us to understand the basics about how mental processes work, and some of the basics about why they work in the way that they do. But as well as providing answers, their findings continue to raise questions. If memory is an activity not a repository, then how do we understand its dynamics? Why do intelligent beings use so many illogical ways of thinking and reasoning? Can we simulate these to create artificially 'intelligent' machines that do not just process prodigious quantities of information in record time, but also help us to understand other, more human, aspects of mental life? How can we understand the processes involved in creative or non-verbal thinking and communication? What is the precise nature of the relationships between language and thought and between thoughts and feelings? How do people change their minds? Or modify outdated or unhelpful patterns of thinking? We know that answers to these questions, and many more like them, will be complex as so many factors influence psychological aspects of functioning, but as increasingly powerful techniques of research and analysis are being developed, and as relevant variables are sorted from irrelevant ones, answers become increasingly likely.

A surprising amount of psychologists' work has been stimulated by the social and political problems of the twentieth century. For example, strides were made in the understanding and measurement of intelligence and personality during the Second World War, when the armed forces needed better means of recruitment and selection. The behaviour of people in wartime provoked Milgram's famous studies on obedience. Social deprivation in large cities provided the context for the Headstart project, from which we have learned about compensating for environmental disadvantages in early childhood. Developing business as well as political cultures provide the context for studies of leadership, team working, and goal setting. Obvious social problems have produced an urgent need to understand more about prejudice and about how to deal with the stresses and strains of modern life. It is likely that the development of psychology in the next century will continue to be influenced by the social and environmental problems we face. At present, psychologists are still working to understand more about the effects of traumatic experiences on memory, and on the determinants of different types of forgetting and 'recovering' memories, and in areas like this one, partial answers are more common than complete ones. The product of research is often to refine the questions that guide future hypotheses.

Today psychology is a far more diverse subject than it was even fifty years ago, as well as a more scientific one. Its complexity means that it may never develop as a science with a single paradigm, but will continue to provide an understanding of mental life from many different perspectives—cognitive and behavioural, psychophysiological, biological, and social. Like any other discipline, it is the site of conflicting theories as well as agreement, which makes it an exciting discipline within which to work. For example, the more experimental and the more humanistic branches of psychology separated long ago, and have largely developed separately. Perhaps one of the more exciting challenges for psychologists today is in bringing together the products of some of its different specializations. This kind of endeavour has contributed to the development of 'cognitive science', in which scientists from many different fields, not just psychology, are now working together to further our understanding of mental functions—of brain *and* behaviour. Psychologists have always been interested in the biological basis of human life and behaviour, and are now contributing to a developing understanding of how genes and the environment—nature and nurture—interact.

Similarly, close collaboration between research psychologists and their clinical colleagues opens up exciting possibilities. To mention just two of these: advances in the scientific understanding of the developing relationship between an infant and its care-giver could potentially clarify how attachment patterns may set a person on a certain (measurable) pathway which makes subsequent psychopathology more or less likely. Early claims that were once not testable are becoming so as different branches of psychology come together and the people working in them learn from each other. Second, theoretical models which illuminate the relationships between four main aspects of human functioning, thoughts, feelings, bodily sensations, and behaviour, are being constructed taking into account the observations made in the clinic. These complex models have implications not just for understanding mental processes and the determinants of present behaviour, but also for explaining the influence of past experiences and for improved treatments for psychological problems. Undoubtedly future research will raise as many questions as it answers and, equally certainly, psychology will continue to fascinate people—those who know about it only from their own subjective experience as well as those who make it their life's work.

A Selection of Further Reading

Introductory books

These introductory texts are for those who are beginning to develop an interest in psychology whether or not they are still at school. Most of them provide a general overview and the book by Richard Gross, on *Key Studies in Psychology,* is recommended because it gives detailed summaries of thirty-five original articles. These give readers an immediate impression of the scientific material on which psychology is based and a sense of the excitement that comes with the process of discovery.

Eysenck, M. W. (1994). *Perspectives on Psychology.* Hove, Lawrence Erlbaum Associates.

Gross. R. D. (1994). *Key Studies in Psychology* (2nd edition). London, Hodder & Stoughton.

Hayes, N. (1994). *Teach Yourself Psychology.* London, Hodder Headline plc; Licolnwood, Ill., NTC Publishing Group.

Wade, C., and Tavris, C. (1997). *Psychology in Perspective* (2nd edition). New York, Addison Wesley.

Textbooks for students of psychology

These textbooks provide more detail about all of the main areas studied in psychology, and are a selection of those recommended by teachers of undergraduate psychology courses. They are all well-organized books that students have found enjoyable as well as informative, and which include up-to-date material.

Atkinson, R. L., Atkinson, R. C., Smith, E. E., Bem, D. J., and Nolen-Hoeksma, S. (1996). *Introduction to Psychology* (12th edition). Orlando, Fla., Harcourt Brace & Co.

Bowlby, J. (1997). *Attachment and Loss* (vol i, 2nd edition). London, Century.

Butterworth, G., and Harris, M. (1995). *Principles of Developmental Psychology.* Hove, Lawrence Erlbaum Associates.

Coolican, H. (lead author) (1996). *Applied Psychology.* London, Hodder & Stoughton.

Eysenck, M. W. (1993). *Principles of Cognitive Psychology*. Hove, Lawrence Erlbaum Associates.

Gleitman, H. (1995). *Psychology* (4th edition). New York, W. W. Norton & Co.

Green, D. W., and others (1996). *Cognitive Science: An Introduction*. Oxford, Blackwell Publishing Inc.

Groeger, J. A. (1997). *Memory and Remembering*. Edinburgh, Addison Wesley Longman.

Gross, R. D. (1996). *Psychology: The Science of Mind and Behaviour* (3rd edition). London, Hodder & Stoughton.

Kalat, J. W. (1995). *Biological Psychology* (5th edition). Pacific Grove, Calif., Brooks/Cole Publishing Co.

Lord, C. G. (1997). *Social Psychology*. Orlando, Fla.; Holt, Reinhart & Winston.

Oatley, K., and Jenkins, J. M. (1996). *Understanding Emotions*. Oxford, Blackwell Publishing Inc.

Schaffer, H. R. (1996). *Social Development*. Oxford, Blackwell Publishing Inc.

Sternberg, R. J. (1996). *Cognitive Psychology*. Orlando, Fla.; Holt, Reinhart & Winston.

Storr, A. (1992). *The Art of Psychotherapy*. London, Butterworth Heinemann.

Wade C., and Tavris, C. (1993). *Psychology* (3rd edition). New York, HarperCollins.

Weiskrantz, L. (1997). *Consciousness Lost and Found*. Oxford, Oxford University Press.

Westen, D. (1996). *Psychology: Mind, Brain and Culture*. New York, John Wiley & Sons.

Books written for the general public

Psychology has always been of general interest, and there are many excellent books which make the subject accessible and interesting to those who are curious about some aspect of the way in which the mind works. Those listed here have been chosen because they are easy to read, useful, or of special interest.

Baddeley, A. (1996). *Your Memory: A User's Guide* (3rd edition). London, Prion.

Butler, G., and Hope, T. (1995). *Manage Your Mind: The Mental Fitness Guide*. Oxford, Oxford University Press.

Frankl, V. (1959). *Man's Search for Meaning*. New York, Pocket Books.

Goleman, D. (1996). *Emotional Intelligence*. London, Bloomsbury.

Gregory, R. L. (1997). *Eye and Brain: The Psychology of Seeing* (5th edition). Oxford, Oxford University Press.

Lorenz, K. (1996). *On Aggression*. London, Routledge. (First published in 1963.)

Luria, A. R. (1968). *The Mind of the Mnemonist* (trans. L. Soltaroff). New York, Basic Books.

Myers, D. G. (1992). *The Pursuit of Happiness*. New York, Avon Books

Ornstein, R. (1991). *The Evolution of Consciousness: The Origins of the Way We Think*. New York, Touchstone.

Sacks, O. (1985). *The Man Who Mistook His Wife for a Hat*. London, Gerald Duckworth & Co. Ltd. (Picador, 1986)

Sutherland, S. (1992). *Irrationality: The Enemy Within*. London, Penguin Books.

Index

OXFORD

MORE OXFORD PAPERBACKS

This book is just one of nearly 1000 Oxford Paperbacks currently in print. If you would like details of other Oxford Paperbacks, including titles in the World's Classics, Oxford Reference, Oxford Books, OPUS, Past Masters, Oxford Authors, and Oxford Shakespeare series, please write to:

UK and Europe: Oxford Paperbacks Publicity Manager, Arts and Reference Publicity Department, Oxford University Press, Walton Street, Oxford OX2 6DP.

Customers in UK and Europe will find Oxford Paperbacks available in all good bookshops. But in case of difficulty please send orders to the Cash-with-Order Department, Oxford University Press Distribution Services, Saxon Way West, Corby, Northants NN18 9ES. Tel: 01536 741519; Fax: 01536 746337. Please send a cheque for the total cost of the books, plus £1.75 postage and packing for orders under £20; £2.75 for orders over £20. Customers outside the UK should add 10% of the cost of the books for postage and packing.

USA: Oxford Paperbacks Marketing Manager, Oxford University Press, Inc., 200 Madison Avenue, New York, N.Y. 10016.

Canada: Trade Department, Oxford University Press, 70 Wynford Drive, Don Mills, Ontario M3C 1J9.

Australia: Trade Marketing Manager, Oxford University Press, G.P.O. Box 2784Y, Melbourne 3001, Victoria.

South Africa: Oxford University Press, P.O. Box 1141, Cape Town 8000.

A Very Short Introduction

CLASSICS

Mary Beard and John Henderson

This *Very Short Introduction* to Classics links a
haunting temple on a lonely mountainside to the
glory of ancient Greece and the grandeur of Rome,
and to Classics within modern culture—from Jeffer-
son and Byron to Asterix and Ben-Hur.

'This little book should be in the hands of every
student, and every tourist to the lands of the ancient world . . . a splendid piece of work'
Peter Wiseman
Author of *Talking to Virgil*

'an eminently readable and useful guide to many
of the modern debates enlivening the field . . . the
most up-to-date and accessible introduction available'
Edith Hall
Author of *Inventing the Barbarian*

'lively and up-to-date . . . it shows classics as a
living enterprise, not a warehouse of relics'
New Statesman and Society

'nobody could fail to be informed and enter-
tained—the accent of the book is provocative and
stimulating'
Times Literary Supplement

POLITICS

Kenneth Minogue

Since politics is both complex and controversial it is easy to miss the wood for the trees. In this Very Short Introduction Kenneth Minogue has brought the many dimensions of politics into a single focus: he discusses both the everyday grind of democracy and the attraction of grand ideals such as freedom and justice.

'Kenneth Minogue is a very lively stylist who does not distort difficult ideas.'
Maurice Cranston

'a dazzling but unpretentious display of great scholarship and humane reflection'
Professor Neil O'Sullivan, University of Hull

'Minogue is an admirable choice for showing us the nuts and bolts of the subject.'
Nicholas Lezard, *Guardian*

'This is a fascinating book which sketches, in a very short space, one view of the nature of politics . . . the reader is challenged, provoked and stimulated by Minogue's trenchant views.'
Talking Politics

A Very Short Introduction

ARCHAEOLOGY

Paul Bahn

'Archaeology starts, really, at the point when the first recognizable 'artefacts' appear—on current evidence, that was in East Africa about 2.5 million years ago—and stretches right up to the present day. What you threw in the garbage yesterday, no matter how useless, disgusting, or potentially embarrassing, has now become part of the recent archaeological record.'

This Very Short Introduction reflects the enduring popularity of archaeology—a subject which appeals as a pastime, career, and academic discipline, encompasses the whole globe, and surveys 2.5 million years. From deserts to jungles, from deep caves to mountain-tops, from pebble tools to satellite photographs, from excavation to abstract theory, archaeology interacts with nearly every other discipline in its attempts to reconstruct the past.

'very lively indeed and remarkably perceptive . . . a quite brilliant and level-headed look at the curious world of archaeology'
Professor Barry Cunliffe,
University of Oxford

A Very Short Introduction

BUDDHISM

Damien Keown

'Karma can be either good or bad. Buddhists speak of good karma as "merit", and much effort is expended in acquiring it. Some picture it as a kind of spiritual capital—like money in a bank account—whereby credit is built up as the deposit on a heavenly rebirth.'

This Very Short Introduction introduces the reader both to the teachings of the Buddha and to the integration of Buddhism into daily life. What are the distinctive features of Buddhism? Who was the Buddha, and what are his teachings? How has Buddhist thought developed over the centuries, and how can contemporary dilemmas be faced from a Buddhist perspective?

'Damien Keown's book is a readable and wonderfully lucid introduction to one of mankind's most beautiful, profound, and compelling systems of wisdom. The rise of the East makes understanding and learning from Buddhism, a living doctrine, more urgent than ever before. Keown's impressive powers of explanation help us to come to terms with a vital contemporary reality.'
Bryan Appleyard

A Very Short Introduction

JUDAISM

Norman Solomon

'Norman Solomon has achieved the near impossible with his enlightened very short introduction to Judaism. Since it is well known that Judaism is almost impossible to summarize, and that there are as many different opinions about Jewish matters as there are Jews, this is a small masterpiece in its success in representing various shades of Jewish opinion, often mutually contradictory. Solomon also manages to keep the reader engaged, never patronizes, assumes little knowledge but a keen mind, and takes us through Jewish life and history with such gusto that one feels enlivened, rather than exhausted, at the end.'
Rabbi Julia Neuberger

'This book will serve a very useful purpose indeed. I'll use it myself to discuss, to teach, agree with, and disagree with, in the Jewish manner!'
Rabbi Lionel Blue

'A magnificent achievement. Dr Solomon's treatment, fresh, very readable, witty and stimulating, will delight everyone interested in religion in the modern world.'
Dr Louis Jacobs, University of Lancaster

FIXATION - TO BE STUCK
(STUCK) ON A SITUATION
OR CONDITION &
UNABLE TO MOVE
OFF OF IT -
Compulsive &
OPPSESSED TO the
point of Being
Taken over
By the event.

TO pick away at the
SCAB of NEUROSIS
the CONDITION in
A STATE OF NON-
CONFLICT -
(MENTAL CONFLICT
- Psyche BREAKS off (SO TO
SPEAK) in to different
directions one for the
cause the other Against it
setting up A psycho WAR of
two strong polarities - its very
painful Till conflict is Resolved.